WE ARE ALL THE TARGET

WE ARE ALL

*A Handbook of
Terrorism Avoidance and
Hostage Survival*

THE TARGET

Douglas S. Derrer

NAVAL INSTITUTE PRESS
Annapolis, Maryland

The views expressed in this book are those of the author and do not reflect the official policy or position of the Department of the Navy, Department of Defense, or the U.S. Government.

Library of Congress Cataloging-in-Publication Data
Derrer, Douglas S.
    We are all the target : a handbook of terrorism avoidance and hostage survival / Douglas S. Derrer.
        p.   cm.
    Includes bibliographical references and index.
    ISBN 1-55750-150-5 (acid-free paper)
    1. Terrorism—Prevention—Handbooks, manuals, etc. 2. Victims of terrorism—Handbooks, manuals, etc.   I. Title.
HV6431.D47   1992   92-4415
362.88—dc20   CIP

Printed in the United States of America on acid-free paper ∞

9 8 7 6 5 4 3 2

First printing

To my mother,
Patricia (1918–1983),
who was a survivor all her life
and who gave me my earliest and best lessons

Contents

Acknowledgments

Many of my teachers and mentors fostered and encouraged my involvement in terrorism. I am deeply indebted to the late Cassie Wesselius, M.D., psychiatrist and specialist in terrorism, hostage-taking, and negotiation, who nurtured my fledgling interest and brought me into contact with the FBI Academy. There I met several individuals who evolved from colleagues to friends and helped me to understand terrorism from the operational side. Tom Strentz, Ph.D., special agent in charge of the academy's Behavioral Science Unit, engaged me in various field training exercises during which I could observe hostage stress, the Stockholm syndrome, and survival reactions firsthand. At one of these exercises I met another psychologist, Cristina Lawrence, Ph.D., who has deepened my knowledge of the psychological impact of critical incidents and the effectiveness of various coping skills.

Every writer needs friends to fan his or her creative flames, especially when they are burning low. Dr. Strentz and Dr. Lawrence offered me their encouragement and also labored painstakingly through early drafts of this book. I am deeply indebted to them both.

A great deal of my own terrorism training resulted from the strong support I received from two directors of the U.S. Navy's Survival, Evasion, Resistance, and Escape (SERE) School in San Diego, California. Comdr. Ralph Gaither and Comdr. K. O. Moos showed interest in my ideas, and their willingness to permit me to explore many dimensions of this complex field greatly enriched and broadened my knowledge and experience during my tours of duty at SERE.

Many fine teachers have shown me that knowledge is power in an uncertain world. If I can teach others as well, I will be worthy of their trust in me.

WE ARE ALL THE TARGET

Introduction

The world began to show significant changes as it prepared to enter into the final decade of the twentieth century. The former Soviet Union and the United States have withdrawn many of their troops from other countries. In a serious outbreak of peace, a new spirit of East-West cooperation has produced arms reduction treaties—one treaty broke a nine-year stalemate in negotiations. Both East and West are getting rid of nuclear missles. Communist dictatorships have fallen throughout the Eastern bloc and are being replaced with fledgling democracies. Since the fall of the Berlin Wall, Germans on both sides have been working out the problems of reunification. Democratic elections have taken place in Nicaragua, and the Sandinistas have lost. Free-market economics is replacing communism in the former USSR. The Soviets are asking the help of the United States and other Western countries in this transformation; the Cold War is over.

Leaders of the European common market countries met in late 1991 to set initial goals in planning for political and economic unity, open borders, a common currency, and free-market exchange. Armies and navies, both Soviet and American, have been substantially reduced for the first time since the end of World War II. Indeed, peace seems to have broken out nearly everywhere. Perhaps by the year 2000, peace and freedom such as the world has never known will become widespread and commonplace. Many prophets of the "New Age" believe that it is finally arriving. If these changes continue, conventional warfare—huge armies, navies, and air forces pitted against each other with incredibly destructive weapons to achieve military and political ends—may be on its way to extinction.

2

TERRORISM—THE UNCONVENTIONAL WARFARE

A shadow overcasts these hopeful and auspicious signs of increasing world peace. Unconventional warfare or low-frequency, low-intensity conflict is the shadow of terrorism. A small force that undertakes carefully selected killings or kidnappings, combined with the clever, effective use of worldwide electronic media, can exert enormous leverage against a much more powerful enemy.

In spite of the glad tidings about propitious changes taking place in Europe and the Eastern bloc, many troubled, "have-not" nations continue to suffer from internal strife and conflict with their neighbors. Often, these countries have no large armies or powerful weapons but use the more practical and efficient means of waging war through terrorist actions and guerrilla operations. Lebanon, with its seemingly endless battles, is a case in point, as are Bolivia, Colombia, and Peru, with their drug cartels and various guerrilla and terrorist groups. Terrorism is the vanguard of insurgencies around the world—Central and South America, Southeast

Asia, India, Africa, and the Middle East. Insurrections, guerrilla wars, and terrorist actions will hopefully not lead to nuclear holocaust or World War III, but Americans will continue to be affected by them politically, militarily, and sometimes personally as victims.

U.S. citizens have been attacked, killed, or taken hostage **3** in almost all of these places. These actions will increase as the United States becomes more involved in these countries, whether through tourism, education, economic advice, business, political or military assistance, interdiction of drug traffickers, or direct intervention (as in Grenada and Panama). We will continue to subject ourselves to the risk of terrorism and remain vulnerable to terrorist assault.

THE GROWTH OF TERRORISM

Throughout the world, terrorism has been on the increase since the late 1960s, despite numerous counteractions and worldwide diplomatic pressure against state sponsors of terrorism. Brian Michael Jenkins, a terrorism specialist for the RAND Corporation, noted in 1985:

> Overall, the volume of terrorist activity has grown at an annual rate of about 12 to 15 percent. If that rate of increase continues, we could see a doubling of terrorist activity by the end of the decade—not an inconceivable prospect. Several factors suggest the likelihood of continued growth. The increase in the volume of terrorist activity has been matched by the geographic spread of terrorism—a slow, long-term trend.[1]

The political and social changes taking place in Europe will not halt the rise in international terrorism. Political unrest in many areas of the world produces unrelenting frustration and anger, especially among those who, like the Palestinians, feel disenfranchised and unable to get what they want through legitimate political means. These conditions create fertile ground for terrorist ideology and actions.

State support and state sponsorship of terrorism is increasing, particularly in poor and powerless Middle Eastern countries, as an effective means of attracting attention and influencing the United States and its allies. Similar trends are taking place in Latin American countries, which have been responsible for more than 50 percent of all international terrorist incidents during recent years.[2]

The economic and political unification of Europe, with its elimination of travel restrictions and border checkpoints, is a boon to transnational terrorism. It is now easier for groups in different countries to maintain contact and carry out joint operations. The vast system of international arms sales makes the acquisition of weapons, explosives, and specialized ordnance electronics relatively simple for terrorist groups.

Global communication ensures instant worldwide coverage of any terrorist incident. Groups with little or no political legitimacy or military power can anticipate a world forum for the expression of their causes, grievances, and demands. The power of this media publicity alone predicts the continuation and increase of terrorism well into the next century.

Finally, the United States was slow to respond to international terrorism. During the 1970s, when much terrorist activity was taking place in Europe, Americans were relatively unaffected. Europe battled terrorism with changes in political policy, new police and security procedures, and the development of specialized counterterrorist (CT) rescue teams that were spectacularly successful at Entebbe, Mogadishu, and Princess Gate, London. The United States did not take the threat of international terrorism seriously until late in

1979 when our embassy in Tehran was taken and its personnel held hostage. Then, as a nation, we faced the plight of the Iranian hostages on the nightly news for 444 long days and the painful, tragic failure of our own CT rescue team at Desert One. We began seriously to feel something must be done about terrorism.

5

TARGETS OF TERRORISM

We are all targets. Since 1983, terrorist attacks against U.S. targets have comprised about 25 percent of all international terrorist incidents. Attacks against U.S. Department of Defense (DoD) personnel and facilities have been slightly less than 10 percent of the yearly worldwide total.[3]

Incidents such as the *Achille Lauro* episode, the Rome and Vienna airport massacres, the La Belle Disco bombing, the hijacking of TWA flight 847, and the bombing of Pan Am flight 103 over Lockerbie, Scotland, strongly suggest several troublesome trends. As American embassies, corporations, and military bases have upgraded, or hardened, their security, terrorists appear to be attacking softer targets. Attacks against U.S. government personnel and other citizens seem to be on the increase. More spectacular assaults with greater casualties, death, and destruction are also evident.

American citizens make easy targets. Mostly, we are not trained to avoid or prepared to cope with terrorist incidents. Americans are easily recognizable. Our clothes, cars, habits, speech, and styles are widely known. American military personnel abroad are particularly easy terrorist targets. Although bases are readily identifiable and have been hit, they are usually more secure. Military personnel, however, are more often targeted while going to work or traveling, or when they are at leisure or on liberty.

Americans are easily accessible targets. More than a million Americans, including government officials, business people, tourists, and deployed military, are overseas at any one time and are particularly sought after by terrorist groups for several reasons. Americans are symbolic targets. We represent the U.S. government and its values, prestige, presence, and power throughout the world. When U.S. citizens are victims of a hijack or are assaulted or killed, our government's reaction brings much attention and publicity to the group responsible for the act. This in turn makes us all the more desirable as convenient, opportune targets for terrorists who want to make anti-American statements or to attract the attention of our government. Becoming a terrorist victim is increasingly likely.

But the victim is not the target. The real target of a terrorist attack is the rest of us. The primary goal of a terrorist attack is to achieve widespread media publicity. Terrorists make every effort to broadcast their actions to the largest possible audience. Terrorists seek to impress, influence, or propagandize the larger audience of American citizens, the U.S. government, the military, or world public opinion. Because of the effectiveness of such tactics, terrorists will continue to hit U.S. citizens and American business and military targets to obtain the notoriety, publicity, and psychological and political impact they seek.

A long and tragic chapter in U.S. history, American victimization by terrorists antedates the presidency of George Washington.[4] (For example, the hostage-taking episodes of the Barbary Coast pirates victimized several hundred Americans.) A review of just a few incidents during the past dozen years illustrates how we continue to be victims of this undeclared, seemingly endless, clandestine war.

A Terrorism "Hit List" of American Targets

- Belgium, June 1979—Gen. Alexander Haig, Supreme Allied Commander of Europe, narrowly missed death when a bomb detonated by the German Red Army Faction (RAF) nearly destroyed his staff car.
- Tehran, November 1979—For the second time that year, Iranian "students" stormed the U.S. Embassy and held fifty-two civilians and some military personnel as hostages for 444 days.
- Puerto Rico, December 1979—While driving to work in a Navy van, two sailors were killed and ten wounded by automatic weapons fire from a local terrorist group, the Macheteros, who were Cuban-trained and equipped with AK-47s.
- Heidelberg, September 1981—Gen. F. J. Kroesen, Commander in Chief, U.S. Army, Europe, and his wife were attacked by the German RAF with a rocket-propelled grenade. The missile passed entirely through the general's armored car, missed him and his wife by about six inches, and buried itself in the ground without detonating.
- Verona, Italy, December 1981—Brig. Gen. James Dozier, U.S. Army, was abducted from his home by the Red Brigades and held for forty-three days in a "people's prison" until he was successfully rescued by the Italian Federal Police and the American FBI.
- Puerto Rico, May 1982—Four sailors from the USS *Pensacola* on liberty in uniform in San Juan were machinegunned in the street by the Macheteros. One man died, and the other three were seriously injured.
- Beirut, April 1983—The first suicide truck bombing by Islamic Jihad at the U.S. Embassy killed sixty-three persons (seventeen Americans) and injured more than one hundred.

• San Salvador, May 1983—Lt. Comdr. Al Schaufelberger, U.S. Navy SEAL and a military advisor to the Salvadoran government, was killed by the Popular Liberation Front, the action arm of the Frente Farabundo Martí para Liberación Nacional (FMLN), the Salvadoran insurgents.

• Beirut, October 1983—A suicide truck bomb attack on their barracks killed 241 Marines. The Free Islamic Revolutionary Movement and Islamic Jihad claimed responsibility.

• Beirut, September 1984—The second suicide bombing by Islamic Jihad at the U.S. Embassy killed fourteen persons, including two American servicemen.

• Beirut, June 1985—U.S. Navy Petty Officer Robert Stethem was beaten and shot during the hijacking of TWA flight 847 by two Hezbollah (Party of God) terrorists. About forty civilian passengers and the crew were held hostage for two weeks by Hezbollah and the Amal militia.

• San Salvador, June 1985—Four U.S. Embassy Marine guards and twelve civilians were machine-gunned to death in Chili's Bar by Mardoqueo Cruz, the assault arm of the FMLN.

• Mediterranean Sea, October 1985—Palestinian terrorists hijacked the cruise ship *Achille Lauro* and killed an older passenger in a wheelchair.

• Rome and Vienna airports, December 1985—In simultaneous attacks, the Middle Eastern terrorist Abu Nidal Organization fired automatic weapons at civilians in the ticket areas of the two airports. Sixteen people were killed, including five Americans. These attacks suggested that terrorists were moving toward softer, more accessible targets.

• Berlin, April 1986—A bomb, exploding on the crowded dance floor of La Belle Disco, killed three and wounded more than two hundred persons. Two of the dead and sixty of the injured were U.S. soldiers. The United States launched an air strike against Libya in retaliation.

• Philippines, October 1987—Three Air Force personnel were murdered near Clark Air Force Base by "sparrow squads" of the New People's Army (NPA). In 1974, the NPA had killed three Navy personnel.

• Athens, 1988—U.S. Navy Capt. William Nordeen was killed when a car bomb was detonated by the 17 November Organization. This group had shot and killed U.S. Navy Capt. George Tsantes in 1983 and CIA station chief Richard Welch in 1975.

• Lockerbie, Scotland, December 1988—Guardians of the Islamic Revolution claimed responsibility for the bomb that destroyed Pan Am flight 103, killing 259 passengers and 11 persons on the ground.

• Manila, April 1989—U.S. Army Col. Nick Rowe, who had survived five years as a prisoner of war in South Vietnam, was shot to death by the New People's Army while driving to work.

Terrorism Can Happen to Any of Us—We Are All the Target

This book can save your life. It is not designed just for terrorism specialists but is dedicated and directed to everyone who must live, work, and travel in our dangerous modern world. It acquaints you with the psychology of the worldwide terrorist threat. Should you ever have to face that threat, it provides information from the best civilian and military resources that will improve your chances for survival.

Security and safety are responsibilities of the individual. Embassies, military bases, corporations, and other organizations can provide circumscribed areas of security, but expericnce has shown that most terrorist victims are assaulted, assassinated, or taken hostage when they are away from secure areas. The strategies offered in this book can help you avoid a terrorist attack.

The first chapter gives detailed instructions, developed from experience and research, about personal protection and security. If you should be taken hostage, this guidance can help you to survive your ordeal. Chapter 2 reviews Department of Defense guidelines for military members who become detainees of hostile governments or ideological terrorists and contains much useful information for civilians as well. Chapters 3 and 4 provide a detailed analysis of a hostage-taking scenario. They direct the captive to specific behaviors that will enhance the chance of survival. Terrorism around the globe and throughout history is discussed in Chapter 5. A comprehensive picture of the diverse nature and some psychological aspects of terrorism are presented. The final chapter considers the major issues regarding the future of terrorism and its impact on society and democratic institutions.

This book gives a broad overview of modern terrorism. It is intended to equip the individual, whether civilian or military, with the necessary information, knowledge, and skills to understand this social problem and to cope with it effectively as a potential victim. We must always remember that we are all the targets of terrorism. Everyone needs to know how to survive this threat with honor, integrity, and dignity.

CHAPTER 1

Personal Protection and Security

"An ounce of prevention . . ." is often good advice. In the case of dealing with a terrorist attack, avoidance is clearly the best policy. A primer of rules for personal protection and security can come from many sources, but the simplest three rules are (1) be alert, (2) be unpredictable, and (3) keep a low profile.[1] This chapter considers each of these rules and offers additional advice on automobile, travel, and home security.

This guidance is provided to increase personal security if you travel or live in a hostile area where there is risk of terrorist assault. The majority of terrorist attacks occur when victims are traveling or at leisure. Intended victims are most vulnerable when traveling, even if they are in armored vehicles as were Generals Haig and Kroesen when they were attacked (see the terrorism "hit list" in the introduction). Clubs, bars, and restaurants that are popular with Americans or military personnel are favorite places for bombings and other assaults. The "hit list" shows the considerable number of assaults and bombings that took place in clubs during leisure time. Americans least expect to be attacked when relaxing and having a good time. Terrorists know that and take advantage of this vulnerability.

In a high-threat area, military personnel know that bases, squadrons, and ships provide good security, and they can usually feel safe when at work. Some European bases were hit with terrorist attacks in the 1970s and early 1980s. As these bases became hardened targets and less accessible, terrorists started to hit military personnel and other Americans when they were away from the protective enclosure of their bases, particularly when they were traveling or at leisure. Consequently, it can be lifesaving to know the principles of personal protection and to apply them on a day-to-day basis.

Often, Americans are cautious for awhile, but the lack of any terrorist action may lull them into complacency and a false sense of security. This, of course, is exactly what terrorists want. During this lull, they may be surveilling their targets, setting them up, and planning the assault. Terrorists frequently take advantage of their targets' complacency and predictability.

To avoid becoming another terrorist victim, learn and follow the three primary rules for personal protection outlined below. Appropriate measures for automobile, airline, and home security are also listed. You are also strongly advised to obtain additional, detailed information on the nature of the threat from reliable security sources before you leave home and when you arrive at your overseas destination.[2]

PERSONAL SECURITY

Be Alert

- Get up-to-date information on the local threat from your intelligence officer or security specialist. Ask about terrorist groups, their targets, their modus operandi, their treatment of hostages, the location of dangerous areas, and the like.

• Read local newspapers. Take rumors and stories seriously; they provide a great deal of useful information, even when they are exaggerated or distorted. Information that is familiar to the local people may be novel to you, so keep your eyes and ears open.

• Observe for surveillance. If you find evidence of it, alert security. Most terrorist attacks are carefully planned and their targets are watched. Do not brush off suspected surveillance as paranoia. In a high-threat area, it is beneficial to be alert.

• Do not open unfamiliar or suspicious letters or parcels. Be wary of excessive postage, no return address, titles rather than names used, presence of stains, or protruding wires. Receive mail at your office. If doubtful about a letter or package, alert security personnel and let them handle it.

• Brief your family and hired help about the threat and have a response plan. Too often we try to protect family members by not alerting them to the potential dangers of living overseas. Should something go wrong, they will not be prepared or know how to act. (See the section on home security about establishing a "safe haven.")

Be Unpredictable

• Vary routines, schedules, and regular habits. This tactic is especially important if you are required to be at work at prescribed times. Terrorists take advantage of such predictable factors. In 1984, William Buckley, the CIA station chief in Beirut, was taken hostage and later tortured and killed. Although an intelligence expert, Buckley refused to vary the route he traveled to work.[3] Also vary your times and routes to and from meetings, church, and regular appointments.

- Vary other activities, such as shopping, yard work, and physical exercise.
- Advise your family to use unpredictable patterns as well.

14 Keep a Low Profile

- Avoid crowds, demonstrations, and riots, even if they are not specifically anti-American. It is possible to get caught up in mob behavior and become an innocent bystander.
- Avoid public places popular with Americans and do not cluster with other Americans. Understandably, you may enjoy being with others from home, but if you know where Americans can be found so do the terrorists. Terrorists sometimes set their bombs or make their attacks in the same clubs to kill and injure Americans.
- Do not reveal your job or advertise your military membership to others who do not have a definite need to know.
- Do not wear distinctively American clothing or jewelry.
- Do not wear your uniform off base unless required.
- Blend into the local community. Learn and use at least some of the local language, customs, and habits.

AUTOMOBILE SECURITY

- Get a local, unobtrusive car and license plates. Keep the car locked and garaged, if possible, when not in use.
- Keep any necessary vehicle passes or decals in the car and present them only when required.
- Always lock your car and inspect it on your return. Check the undercarriage, wheel wells, and exhaust pipes. If anything appears suspicious, alert security or the police.
- Practice defensive driving mentally. Anticipate problems and how to evade them. Many foreign cities have nar-

row, crooked streets and high curbs. If you practice evasion in your mind while you drive, you will be better prepared if interdicted by terrorists.

• If followed or attacked while in your car, do not drive home. Know the locations of police stations, military bases, hospitals, and government buildings and try to reach the nearest one.

15

• If you are shot at while driving, stay as low as you can and try to get far away as quickly as possible. The "kill zone" in most terrorist attacks is usually quite narrow, so you may not have far to go to escape.

• Do not try to escape if you are stopped and terrorists actually have their hands on you. This is not the time to be a hero. The terrorists will be tense, anxious, and possibly trigger happy. By trying to escape at this point, you may inadvertently turn a kidnapping into a killing.

AIRLINE SECURITY

• Keep travel plans private; advise no one of your plans except those with a need to know. Check in regularly with your office or home. Should you be taken hostage, the authorities will know where to begin their search.

• Travel in nondistinctive civilian clothes whenever possible.

• Do not loiter in public areas in airports. Terrorist incidents are more likely to occur in these areas.

• Proceed quickly through security checks to the more secure boarding area.

• Do not agree to watch or to carry onto aircraft any briefcases, luggage, or packages for strangers. Report such requests to airport security.

• Do not discuss your position, job, or military membership with others.

• Avoid arguments with other passengers. You may need allies later if there is a hijacking, or they could be terrorists.

• Obtain a tourist passport to present as identification to a hijacker rather than your diplomatic passport or military identification. Avoid giving hijackers identification that marks you as someone important or special.

• Limit the number of documents on your person and be prepared to explain all documents in your possession.

• Avoid carrying classified materials. Mail them in advance in accordance with proper security regulations.

• Locate a "stash area" on the aircraft to hide your identification and any documents, if needed, such as beneath the removable seat cushions.

• Do not carry reading matter that a terrorist might regard as decadent or provocative, such as *Soldier of Fortune*, *Hustler*, or similar publications that could incite violence.

• Dress up your wallet with pictures of a spouse and children, even if you are not married. This can be helpful in dealing with some terrorists (e.g., Middle Eastern) who may respond more favorably to persons with families.

HOME SECURITY

• When choosing a residence, consider whether a house or a well-managed apartment with controlled access to the building is more secure.

• Get acquainted with neighbors, and make mutual security plans with them. Be suspicious of strangers; they might be engaged in surveillance.

• Get background checks on all local persons working for you in the home. You want to avoid hiring a terrorist gardener or maid.

• Have security personnel inspect your office and quarters and make recommendations to prevent intruders. Pre-

16

cautions and security procedures to deter thieves may also keep out a terrorist.

• Do not attempt to confront or apprehend an intruder. Call the authorities.

• Establish a "safe haven" within your home. It should be a secure room, such as a bedroom or bathroom, that has a solid door. Keep a telephone and radio there, along with flashlights and rations. If something untoward does happen, the family can go to this secure area and call for help.

17

• Do not unwittingly divulge useful information over the telephone; brief your family, especially children and hired help.

• Maintain careful control of keys, especially with children and those working for you in the home.

• Do not admit strangers to your quarters. Persons seeking entry should be fully identified and the reason for their visit verified. Brief your hired help.

• Keep bushes and hedges cut low for better outside visibility and fewer hiding places.

• Install outside floodlights.

• Keep your yard clean to avoid booby traps.

• A dog is the single best security system.

PREPARATION FOR OVERSEAS DEPARTURE

Almost without exception, prisoners of war (POWs) and hostages who took the time to put their house in order prior to captivity fared much better psychologically than those who did not. Usually, there is ample time in captivity to dwell upon and worry about all the complex problems that your absence has caused, especially for your family and loved ones. Face the very unpleasant fact, now, that you might be taken hostage and be away for a long time, or never return.

You should seriously consider the applicable legal, financial, medical, family, and personal issues included in the predeparture and family preparation checklists below. Have an open, candid discussion with your spouse about what should be done if the worst-case scenario occurs. If it does and you have dealt with these issues, you will have much greater peace of mind about your family's welfare.

18
___

Predeparture Checklist

_____ A safe repository in the United States for the *originals* of all your important papers, such as medical and dental records, school records, birth and death certificates, mortgages, tax records, and insurance papers.

_____ *Legal copies* (three each to be kept at the family residence) of any of the following: birth certificates of all family members, marriage certificate, divorce decree, death certificate of former spouse, adoption papers, and other important documents.

_____ Power of attorney for each responsible adult family member. Do you have your spouse's power of attorney? Make several copies of each and keep them in safe places at home.

_____ Up-to-date wills for you and your spouse. Wills should provide for common disaster. Your attorney or executor should have copies.

_____ Various credit cards with adequate available credit for your spouse to use in emergencies.

_____ Current Record of Emergency Data (for military personnel).

_____ Current and correct insurance policies (e.g., proper beneficiaries designated; war clauses; restrictions that limit mode of payments; extended term insurance).

_____ Joint checking account that you or your spouse can use if you are separated.

_____ Current social security card for your spouse.

_____ Information about benefits your dependents will receive from the Department of Veterans Affairs and Social Security Administration in the event of your death or disability. Are they aware of these benefits?

19

_____ Information about how much income your dependents will receive from your life insurance and how the benefits will be paid. Is your family aware of this information? You may wish to consider establishing a trust fund for your dependents.

_____ A plan to coordinate all your benefits.

_____ Complete and up-to-date medical and dental checkups. Do not leave home with an unfilled cavity. Are you in good physical condition?

_____ Adequate supplies of medications you and your dependents require. Carry a small supply with you at all times.

_____ Familiarity with exercise programs that require little space, such as yoga, isometrics, calisthenics, or the Royal Canadian Air Force exercise program.

_____ Enough knowledge of the language spoken at your destination to help you in an emergency.

Family Preparations Checklist

Hold personal discussions with your family concerning any of the following matters that apply.

_____ Actions your family will take if you are captured. Will they leave the country? Where will they go (back to parents, friends, or relatives)?

_____ Provisions to support the family (e.g., paychecks sent directly to your bank account).

20

_____ Provisions to continue a family-owned business in your absence.

_____ Family resources for support, guidance, and therapy (e.g., spiritual, mental, financial, legal, occupational, or educational counseling). Your family should be familiar with any of the following resources that apply:

- commanding officer, ombudsman, and other military resources
- civilian attorney or legal officer
- chaplain, pastor, or casualty affairs officer
- Red Cross, Department of Veterans Affairs, Navy Relief, Fleet Reserve, and other private and government organizations
- organizations for spouses and families of hostages, POWs, and military personnel missing in action (MIA)
- Civilian Health and Medical Program of the Uniformed Services (CHAMPUS) and other insurance for medical and psychological treatment.

You and your family should consider the following issues that could arise as a result of your capture or death:

_____ Children's emotional problems.

_____ Children's education—schools, college savings, future plans.

_____ The people who will care for the children if both parents are captured or killed (relatives, parents, godparents, or friends).

_____ Increased independence of spouse as he or she assumes the total responsibility of making decisions, disciplining children, and handling family finances.

_____ Role adjustments of family members. Your tasks and responsibilities must be reallocated among other family members.

_____ Coping strategies to help family members adjust to the ordeal. It can be helpful if they undertake productive activities that enhance their self-esteem and occupy them mentally and emotionally, as well as engage in recreation and leisure activities that offer satisfying outlets.

21

_____ Long-term hostage POW/MIA status. Should your spouse wait out the ordeal, see if you appear on hostage or POW lists or divorce and perhaps remarry?

_____ Reactions of family members to hostage or POW statements. They should not believe all they see or hear or be too optimistic or too pessimistic.

_____ Correspondence. Consider the following:

• Letters will be short and probably censored.

• The family should show all letters to the Department of State or the Department of Defense to ensure that they are analyzed for possible hidden information.

• You may wish to designate codes that can communicate your identity and treatment. Keep the codes simple so they are easily remembered under stress.

• You can devise clues to be used in analyzing your handwriting.

• Clues also can be used to indicate the real conditions and the health and welfare of other POWs or hostages, especially those listed as killed in action (KIA) or MIA.

• Your spouse and other family members should understand the importance of not making public statements on their interpretation of your correspondence.

_____ Ransom considerations if you or your spouse is kidnapped. Family members should abide by the following rules if contacted by captors:

• Contact authorities immediately.

- Do not act as contacts with the hostage-takers.
- Be extremely cautious with the media and appoint some responsible person outside the family to act as a buffer between the family and the media.

_____ Love and appreciation for your family and friends. This is the most important item on your checklist. Your family and friends need to know how much you care for them, and you need to tell them. Regrets can torture a hostage or POW.

22

CHAPTER 2

Military Policy on Peacetime Captivity

All U.S. military personnel are walking symbols of their country and its power, prestige, and presence around the world. They are prime targets of ideological terrorists and of hostile governments that seek media publicity or to influence or embarrass the United States. The worldwide activities and deployments of military personnel place them at constant risk of peacetime captivity as hostages or detainees. Peacetime captivity can occur when the United States is not officially at war with any country. Its demands and difficulties are similar to, but significantly different from, those of being a prisoner of war (POW). All military personnel should know what is expected of them by their government if they are captured in war or peace. Although the following guidance specifies the problems and responsibilities of the potential military captive, civilians will also find the information useful.

As a member of the military, you must overcome your denial and complacency regarding the terrorist threat. You *are* a possible target. Denial means thinking, "It will never happen to me." But it certainly could, particularly when you are away from the protective umbrella of your base, squadron, ship, or post. Most terrorist attacks against military personnel occur when they are traveling or when they are at leisure in a club or recreational facility. Complacency results from believing, "I'm not important enough. I'm not a high ranking person. They wouldn't want me." This is not a rational belief—terrorists have hit all ranks with their hostage-takings and murderous assaults (as shown by the "hit list" in the introduction). Because you symbolize the United States by the uniform you wear, you are important enough.

24

The Code of Conduct for Members of the Armed Forces of the United States[1] exists for your guidance should you become a captive; it applies in peace as well as in war:

CODE OF CONDUCT

I.   I am an American, fighting in the forces which guard my country and our way of life. I am prepared to give my life in their defense.

II.   I will never surrender of my own free will. If in command I will never surrender the members of my command while they still have the means to resist.

III.   If I am captured I will continue to resist by all means available. I will make every effort to escape and aid others to escape. I will accept neither parole nor special favors from the enemy.

IV.   If I become a prisoner of war, I will keep faith with my fellow prisoners. I will give no information or take part in any action which might be harmful to my comrades. If I am senior, I will take command. If not, I will obey the lawful orders of those appointed over me and will back them up in every way.

V.   When questioned, should I become a prisoner of war, I am required to give name, rank,

service number, and date of birth. I will evade an-
swering further questions to the utmost of my ability. I will make no oral or written statements disloyal
to my country and its allies or harmful to their
cause.

VI. I will never forget that I am an American, fighting for freedom, responsible for my actions, and dedicated to the principles which made
my country free. I will trust in my God and in the
United States of America.

25

Be intimately familiar with the code's six articles and,
most importantly, know how it has been effectively applied
by former POWs and other detainees. Every military member has seen the code of conduct and signed a statement to
uphold it "to the utmost of my ability."[2] But few persons
receive additional or advanced training in application of the
code unless they are at high risk of capture in combat or their
missions take them "in harm's way." These personnel attend
Survival, Evasion, Resistance and Escape (SERE) schools
where they receive special training to resist enemy interrogation, torture, exploitation for propaganda, and the duress of
captivity.[3] Because of the demanding nature of SERE schools
and the specialized groups they serve, not everyone is able to
attend. Yet all personnel in uniform are potential targets of
terrorist attack or of detention by a hostile foreign power.
For your own safety and protection, it is vital to know and
understand the code and also to be familiar with Department
of Defense (DoD) Directive 1300.7, which provides guidance
for various forms of captivity.[4]

The essence of this policy is: "U.S. military personnel
isolated from U.S. control are required to do everything in
their power to follow DoD policy. The DoD policy in this
situation is to *survive with honor*"[5] (emphasis added). It is

important to understand thoroughly what your government expects of you in these situations. Explication of the DoD policy on peacetime captivity is provided in three sections: (1) general guidance, (2) guidance for detention by hostile governments, and (3) guidance for captivity by ideological terrorists. Your responsibilities as a military person under the Code of Conduct and the DoD policy are not easy. Conducting yourself properly while being held captive during peacetime, either by an unfriendly government or by terrorists, could be the most demanding duty you will ever have.

GENERAL GUIDANCE

Faith

"Faith in one's country and its way of life, faith in fellow detainees or captives, and faith in one's self are critical to surviving with honor and resisting exploitation."[6] This statement echoes Article IV of the Code of Conduct and is one of the most important concepts for captives to maintain. Captors try especially to break down faith in country and fellow prisoners. They often play captives against each other, divide them, and provide captives with different slanted and incomplete information or outright lies. Keeping faith, maintaining unity, and pulling together are major sources of strength and resistance for all captives.

DOD policy states: "U.S. military personnel, whether detainees or captives, may be assured that the U.S. Government shall make every good faith effort to obtain their earliest release."[7] It offers assurance to captives that they will not be forgotten and that their families will be cared for. Since Vietnam, our country has shown its concern for possible POWs and MIAs in Southeast Asia. When American hostages are taken in the Middle East, the United States maintains a vigil for their safe return as well.

Resistance to Exploitation

"Every reasonable step must be taken by U.S. military personnel to prevent exploitation of themselves and the U.S. Government. If exploitation may not be prevented completely, every step must be taken to limit the exploitation as much as possible."[8]

Military personnel who are captured or detained by hostile foreign governments or terrorists are often subjected to attempts at exploitation. Detainees have been exploited for information and propaganda, including confessions of crimes never committed, to assist or lend credibility to the detainer. This policy guidance is intended solely to help U.S. military personnel survive captivity with honor. It does not constitute a means for judgment or replace the Uniform Code of Military Justice (UCMJ).

The American public consistently shows intense interest in the welfare of U.S. citizens who have been taken prisoner by hostile governments or terrorists. This humanitarian concern, however, makes Americans more vulnerable as hostage targets because they are used for propaganda by those seeking illegitimate media access to herald their particular causes. Military detainees must limit, as much as possible, the extent to which they contribute to such publicity and exploitation for propaganda purposes. The Code of Conduct prescribes a resistance posture that is relevant and appropriate in peacetime captivity, and the DoD policy adds some permissible topics that can be discussed with detainers.

Military Bearing

"Regardless of the type of detention or captivity, or harshness of treatment, U.S. military personnel shall maintain their military bearing. They should make every effort to remain calm, courteous, and project personal dignity."[9] Discourteous, unmilitary behavior can result in unnecessary punishment. It may jeopardize survival and severely complicate efforts to gain release of military personnel. A proper military manner may actually elicit respect and better treatment from a captor.

28

Classified Information

"To the utmost of their ability, U.S. military personnel held as detainees, captives or hostages shall protect all classified information."[10] Every attempt by captors to obtain classified information must be resisted.

Chain of Command

"In group detention, captivity, or hostage situations, military detainees, captives, or hostages shall organize, to the fullest extent possible, in a military manner under the senior military member present and eligible to command."[11] Their instructions include the following:

• Every effort must be made to establish a chain of command and maintain communication with other detainees. Communication is vital to survival and morale. It assists detainees in getting a better picture of the situation, supporting each other, and maintaining coherent and consistent relations with the captor.

• Civilian captives must be encouraged to participate in the military organization and accept the authority of the senior military member. Usually, civilians are willing to defer to the military in captivity because they realize that military personnel are trained and better prepared for this type of situation.

• Even if military personnel are under the direction of a senior U.S. civilian official, such as an ambassador in charge of personnel on embassy duty, the ranking military member is obligated to establish a military organization and ensure that DoD policy guidelines to survive with honor are not compromised.

29

GUIDANCE FOR DETENTION BY HOSTILE GOVERNMENTS

Imagine this worst-case scenario: You are flying in a civilian aircraft over the Mediterranean Sea. The aircraft loses power in two of its three engines. The pilot declares an emergency and lands the plane safely in Libya. You and your fellow passengers are taken into custody by Moammar Gadhafi's security police. It is peacetime, but you are now detained by a hostile foreign power. What do you need to know, and what should you do?

It is most important for you to know that you are subject to the civil laws of the government holding you, regardless of the circumstances that led to your detention. Avoid any aggressive, combative, or illegal behavior because it can complicate your situation, your legal status, and efforts to negotiate your release. Maintain your military bearing, dignity, courtesy, and self-control.

If in detention by a hostile government, you should:

• Ask immediately and continually, if necessary, to see U.S. Embassy personnel or a representative of an allied or neutral government.

• Provide your name, rank, social security number, and date of birth. Limit further discussion to (1) the innocent circumstances that led to your detention, (2) health and welfare matters, (3) the conditions of your fellow detainees, and

(4) your release. To generate propaganda and to intimidate or compromise the detainees, captors have sometimes tried to engage in a *battle of wits* with them. It can range from seemingly innocuous conversations to extensive discussions of American values, politics, and policies. Try, instead, to make this a *battle of wills* and keep such discussions short, businesslike, to the point, and on authorized subjects.

• Avoid signing any documents or making any oral or written statements. If forced to make statements or sign documents, provide as little information as possible and continue to resist to the utmost of your ability. *Detainees are not likely to earn their release by cooperation with their captors.* When they realize that you are not going to cooperate willingly, your value as a propaganda source declines and the likelihood of your release increases.

• Consider escape plans carefully. Article III of the Code of Conduct enjoins POWs to ". . . make every effort to escape and aid others to escape." The DoD policy cautions peacetime detainees to consider escape plans carefully because of the risk of violence, the possibility of failure, and the detrimental effect a successful escape could have on the detainees who remain. Remember, jailbreak in most countries is illegal and their civil laws apply to you. The detainer could use an escape attempt to justify bringing you to trial, prolonging your detention, and even injuring or killing you. There is little the United States can legally do to help you in this situation.

• Do not act as a combatant in an evasion attempt if you are lost or isolated in a hostile foreign country during peacetime. Because a state of conflict does not exist, you are not protected by the Geneva Conventions.

• Accept release under almost any circumstances. Accept release, not parole, which is release with strings attached (e.g., exploitation, propaganda, or a signed confession or apology). If you are in charge of a group, you may authorize your subordinates to accept release; early release of part of the group is permissible. However, if you feel that accepting release would be detrimental to your country or its allies, you may consider refusing release until conditions change.

31

GUIDANCE FOR CAPTIVITY BY TERRORISTS

Capture by terrorists is generally the least predictable and structured form of peacetime captivity. Hostages play a greater role in determining their own fate, because terrorists expect and receive no rewards for treating you well or even releasing you unharmed. If you are uncertain as to whether your captors are genuine terrorists or government surrogates, assume they are terrorists.

The following guidance is offered:

• If assigned in or traveling through areas of known terrorist activity, exercise prudent anti-terrorism measures to reduce your vulnerability to terrorist attack or capture (see Chapter 1).

• During the initial capture phase, try to remain calm and self-controlled in order to minimize violence and injury (see Chapter 3).

• Develop a rapport with your captors by talking with them, if you can. This makes it more difficult for them to injure or kill you. Surviving terrorist captivity can result from conveying personal dignity and apparent sincerity to captors. You want your captors to see you as a person with human qualities, rather than as a hated military symbol of the U.S. government.

• Project your personal qualities. You are authorized to discuss nonsubstantive topics, such as family, sports, and clothing, with the terrorists. You are encouraged to listen to their feelings about their cause; however, you may never pander, praise, participate in, or debate their cause with terrorists.

- Make every effort to avoid embarrassing the United States or the host government.
- Accept release in accordance with the guidance given in the section above on detention by hostile governments.
- Make an escape attempt if you consider it your only hope. You are authorized to make this attempt. Each situation is different, and you must carefully weigh every aspect of the decision to attempt escape. Detailed intelligence on the local threat can be valuable. Prior knowledge of hostage treatment by various terrorist groups can be a significant factor in making a decision to escape.
- To survive with honor, keep faith with your fellow hostages and conduct yourself according to the highest traditions of the U.S. military service.

CHAPTER 3

Crisis Stages and Hostage Survival

A hostage-taking episode is a crisis. Contrary to popular belief, however, this type of crisis has a known psychology and predictable patterns. Three stages in a hostage-taking incident constitute its most important patterns. Survival can depend largely on how the hostage behaves, or acts, during each of these stages. *Act* is the right term here because the hostage has a particular role to play during each stage of the incident. Playing those roles well and conforming to the situational requirements of each stage can increase the likelihood of getting through this ordeal alive and unharmed.

The three stages of a hostage-taking episode consist of (1) the intimidation stage, (2) the custodial stage, and (3) the resolution stage. The intimidation stage begins with the hijacking or kidnapping and includes that period when the terrorists are taking control and establishing their authority over the hostages. Usually, this is literally the most terrifying and violent stage for the hostages. They constantly fear for their lives and experience a variety of other disturbing emotions.

The custodial stage begins after the terrorists have established control. This stage includes negotiations over the terrorists' demands, the terrorists' attempts to gain publicity, and efforts to free the hostages. Often the longest stage of any incident, the custodial stage is the most important for survival of the hostages. The excitement and fear of the intimidation stage have largely subsided. Hostages usually experience the second stage as a period of boredom and waiting that is punctuated with cycles of hope and despair.

Finally, the incident enters the resolution stage. Whether the incident is resolved peacefully by negotiations or by a tactical strike rescue mission, this stage is the endgame. If a tactical strike is made, the resolution stage may last only moments. A resolution by negotiation, however, could take much longer but be far safer.

THE ROLES OF A HOSTAGE

The hostage must play certain roles that are important, necessary, and specific to each stage. If played properly, these roles can enhance the hostage's chance for survival, improve his or her treatment, and enable the hostage to cope better with the stress of captivity.

Everyone plays various roles in their daily lives—for example, spouse, parent, breadwinner, homemaker, teacher, friend, business person, professional, student, and so on. Most of the behaviors associated with these different roles seem natural and are chosen unconsciously. When thinking back to the time they assumed each of their roles, most people may realize that they were not particularly comfortable or adept in any of them at the beginning. For example, a girl may have some experience caring for younger siblings, but when she grows up and becomes a mother she may be awkward, uncomfortable, and uncertain of this role at first. Her confidence and ability grow until one day she is playing the role of mother naturally with the automatic skill and grace of a practiced Olympic athlete. Although her children may continue to be problematical from time to time, as all children are, the mother now deals with their difficulties much more smoothly and easily than when she was first learning the role. This same growth and learning experience applies to almost any role one plays in life.

35

Effective role playing is vital to success in life. Some psychologists believe that our very sense of self comes from the various roles we play and how well we play them. We are rewarded by society for playing our roles well, and this makes us feel good. Problems result when one does not play a required role well. If a mother does not act her part appropriately, she feels bad and her children suffer. If a businessman does not play his role well in terms of what his company expects of him, he does not succeed and may be fired.

Finally, if a hostage does not properly play the necessary role demanded by each stage of the incident, he or she may be abused or killed. During the hijacking of a Lufthansa jetliner to Mogadishu by Palestinian and German terrorists in October 1977, the captain of the plane was the only hostage who was killed. An analysis of this incident by the FBI Academy's Behavioral Science Unit indicated that the captain had great difficulty relinquishing his role of being in command. The terrorists wanted him to be more submissive to reduce his authority, but he refused. There was much conflict over this issue, and he was eventually killed.[1]

Such direct power struggles over roles can be only futile when the terrorists have the weapons and other lives are at stake. There are times when hostages can assert their power, sometimes quite directly; but knowing when and how is critical. Understanding the stages of an incident and knowing how to play the correct roles during each stage can be vital to survival.

Hostages have three difficult tasks to accomplish in their survival efforts. First, they must control their disruptive emotions of fear and anger. These emotions, although quite normal and expected in this situation, could get them injured or killed if they are expressed or demonstrated. Second, hostages must be aware of the three stages of a hostage-taking episode, the characteristics of each stage, and the shifting from one stage into the next. This awareness depends on shrewd, careful observation of all that is going on around them. Third, they must know what roles to play and how to play them during each stage of captivity.

The captive's primary goal is to develop a more human relationship with the captors, if possible, so that when tensions rise and fall, as they will during the incident, the hostage is less likely to be harmed. For example, terrorists typically make demands and insist that they be met by a certain deadline or a hostage will be killed. When the deadline passes without the demand being met, the terrorists feel frustrated and angry and may become aggressive once again. If the hostage has developed some rapport and a workable relationship with the terrorists, he or she may be able to talk them through their frustrations and defuse their anger. Uli Derickson, senior flight attendant aboard TWA flight 847, was able to do just that after hostage U.S. Navy Petty Officer Robert Stethem was killed. The terrorists were beating and threatening to kill another Navy diver, Clinton Suggs, when she intervened, calmed the terrorists, reasoned with them, talked them out of killing him, and saved the man's life.

Detailed psychological views of the beginning, middle, and end stages of a hostage-taking, kidnapping or hijacking episode are presented below. Through examination of the components of each stage, the operating psychological factors, and the common emotional reactions, the potential hostage can learn how to cope effectively with untoward emotions, as well as the complexities of the situation, and survive with honor.

THE INTIMIDATION STAGE

37

Terrorist Violence and Death

During the beginning, or intimidation, stage of an incident, the single goal of the terrorists is to assert control over the hostages and the situation itself. This period can be quite dangerous for the hostages because the terrorists may be most violent and brutal during their initial effort to gain *rapid* control over the hostages. Most hostages report that this is the most terrifying period of the ordeal. Further, the terrorists are usually highly tense, anxious, agitated, and possibly trigger happy during this period. They must act fast to put their plan into action and to overcome the potential resistance and adverse reactions of the hostages. Any actions or emotions from the hostages that are perceived by the terrorists to counter their establishment of authority and effort to control the situation probably will be dealt with rapidly and severely.

The terrorists may perpetrate acts of violence toward hostages with or without apparent cause. These acts can consist of yelling and screaming, shoving and hitting the hostages, ordering them about, beating them, torturing them, and even murdering them. The terrorists may perform such acts for several reasons: (1) to make the seriousness of what the terrorists are doing vividly apparent to the hostages, (2) to prevent possible counteraction by the hostages, (3) to serve as an example of what can happen if the hostages do not comply,

(4) to reduce their own tensions, or (5) to act out aggressions based on ideological hatred of the hostages. The beating and later shooting of Petty Officer Stethem during the hijacking of TWA flight 847 seems to have been motivated by all of these reasons.

Usually, hostages are killed to enforce the terrorists' authority during the intimidation stage or to increase the pressure on a government to act on their demands or to speed up negotiations during the custodial stage. It sometimes appears that hostages are randomly selected for death. At other times, the choice may be dictated by the identity of the hostage or whether a relationship exists between the hostage and the terrorists. Where there is high anti-American feeling, an American hostage held by such terrorists may be the only requirement for brutality or death. That was apparently the only reason for the torture of two American businessmen and the murder of two others during the hijacking of Kuwaiti flight 221 in December 1984. There may be little a hostage can do to preserve his or her life when singled out as a target of terrorists' ideological hatred and desire for revenge. Yet, others have survived these threats and dangers. Playing the proper role and establishing a relationship with the terrorists can make all the difference, as it did for Gerald Vaders. A Dutch newspaperman, Vaders became a hostage on a train hijacked by South Moluccan terrorists in Bovinsmilde. Although repeatedly threatened with death and tied for hours in the train doorway as a human shield against a rescue attempt, Vaders's relationship with some of the terrorists ultimately saved him when they started killing hostages.[2]

Emotional Reactions and Coping Strategies

Most people tend to react with anger and fear when under severe stress and threat to life. The duress of suddenly finding oneself being kidnapped or taken hostage gives rise to some of the most extreme emotions one can experience. Life-threatening events can evoke a complex series of physiological and psychological reactions known as the *fight-flight response*. This complex response activates the body's programmed reactions to threat, maximally preparing it to fight or flee in order to survive.[3] This powerful survival response works well for animals in the wilderness. For a human in the midst of a hijacking, however, fighting or fleeing may be impossible or highly dangerous.

39

These extreme and disruptive emotions can cause states bordering on panic or "frozen fear." They can push the hostage to sudden actions that would have been precluded by the better judgment of a person in a calmer state of mind. It is easy to react impulsively, take a foolhardy action, and further endanger everyone. Any aggressive actions, real or only apparent, displayed during the intimidation stage very likely will be handled harshly by terrorists. A hostage can appear aggressive even when frozen with fear or in a daze and may stare vacantly at a terrorist without realizing it. Staring is an aggressive act and can result in an aggressive reaction by the terrorist. Keeping the eyes downcast and looking about only surreptitiously, if at all, during this stage reduces risk and attracts less attention.

Emotionally, the fight-flight response is experienced as fear, rage, or a mixture of both. One is pumped up physically and psychologically but impaired mentally. Clear thinking, sensible judgments, and good decision-making are affected. Time distortion may give the illusion of events moving in slow motion or assuming an unreal quality.

Later in this reaction sequence, there follows a period of disbelief, a kind of psychological shock, numbing, and denial: "This can't be happening to me!" Feelings and emotions seem shut off as one watches what is happening with little reaction. This later period of numbness is safer than the fight-flight reaction, with its emotional extremes.

Controlling extreme emotions and refraining from acting on or displaying them during the intimidation stage are crucial to survival. Emotional control is also basic to playing the proper role of a hostage. Psychologists have developed or discovered specific methods that can be used to control rage and fear and to reduce and dissipate them harmlessly. Some of the methods were employed by POWs in Vietnam to help them control their emotional reactions during the severe stresses of extended captivity. Knowing about these methods and learning certain skills to reduce stress can help a hostage to cope with the ordeal and may ultimately save lives.

Restoring or maintaining emotional control will keep intellectual faculties, such as observation and judgment, intact. The hostage likely will continue to feel fear, but it will be manageable. Courage is functioning in spite of fear, not without it; or, as Hemingway put it, courage is grace under pressure. By controlling, but not necessarily eliminating, disruptive emotions, the hostage will be better able to role-play and enhance the chance of survival with honor and dignity.

(Examples of coping techniques, described in Chapter 4, that work well to calm a person during the fight-flight reaction include the physical methods of instant calm breathing, isometric exercises, and progressive muscle relaxation; the cognitive methods of talk down and hypervigilance; the mental methods of thought stopping, dissociation, and observer reaction; and such beliefs as a positive mental attitude, religious values, prayer, and meditation.)

Compliance

The key role for the hostage to play during the intimidation stage is one of outward compliance. To be overtly resistive—or worse, aggressive—during this stage can result in severe, resolute, and brutal punishment. Punishment is exactly what it is, too. Terrorists are likely to punish a hostage in order to stop any behavior that does not conform to the role they expect the "good" hostage to play.

During this stage, each hostage should be overtly compliant, blend with the group, follow instructions of the terrorists, and try not to attract any attention. This is the time to be a "gray person" and maintain a low profile by complying with the orders of the terrorists. To the extent that the hostages are compliant and appear to be passive and nonthreatening, the terrorists' anxieties and tensions will abate more quickly.

It may seem absurd, or even impossible, that hostages should be concerned about the emotions of the terrorists during an event that is probably the most frightening of their lives. Their awareness of the terrorists as people with emotional reactions, however, can reduce the threat for the hostages and begin to establish a communication bridge to the terrorists that can be invaluable during later stages of captivity. When the terrorists perceive that they do have control, that it is unchallenged, and that their operational plan is unfolding with few complications, the intimidation stage will begin to wane and the custodial stage will supervene. The hostages can then make more active efforts to defuse the situation, show more open resistance to the terrorists' controls, begin communication, and hopefully establish a lifesaving rapport with the terrorists.

THE CUSTODIAL STAGE

Emotional Reactions and Coping Strategies

In sharp contrast to the intense emotions experienced by hostages during the intimidation stage, the emotions of the middle stage are most often reported to be boredom and despair. These feelings are especially prevalent during long-term captivity, such as that experienced by Vietnam POWs. The crisis settles into a dull routine. The hostages may know little or nothing about any negotiations in progress, but they begin to lose the paralyzing fear of the first stage. They may begin to talk and to take care of each other. Water and food must be obtained. The old, young, sick, and injured people must be cared for. Toilet functions have to be accomplished. These simple daily acts can become enormously complex and difficult during a hijacking.

If the incident goes beyond several days, just sitting in an airplane and not knowing what is going on in the outside world can make one feel bored, withdrawn, helpless, and despairing. These numbing feelings are occasionally punctuated with moments of hope or fear as minor incidents and actions such as a smile or a harsh look from a terrorist are interpreted to have great import.

After the abject fear and panic of the intimidation stage have subsided, a great deal of anger is felt by some hostages during the custodial stage. Most hostages, however, experience little anger about an incident until it is over and they are once again safe at home. The anger results from feeling outraged at what they have been subjected to—terror, control, brutality, threats, their rights violated, and their plans spoiled. This anger has to be prudently managed by the hostage or expressed in clandestine ways, as passenger Peter Hill did by numerous covert actions against the terrorists throughout the hijacking of TWA flight 847.[4] A direct, angry confrontation with a terrorist usually results in a worse situation for everyone.

Communication

The attitude of terrorists toward hostages is usually emotionally intense but impersonal. Terrorists see the hostages as symbols of the government they hate (e.g., the United States, Israel), the values they despise (e.g, American, imperialistic), the political system they want to attack (e.g., democratic, capitalistic), or the military they are fighting (e.g., the U.S. Marine Corps). To terrorists, hostages are nonpersons— merely symbols of all they want to destroy and a focus for their ideological rage. The hostages are robbed of their essential nature as individuals and are made the symbolic targets of an attack against what the terrorists regard as a larger, but untouchable, evil. Some terrorism specialists believe, for example, that hostage-takers place hoods over the heads of their victims not so much to prevent them from seeing where they are going, but rather to depersonalize them further. It is much easier, psychologically, to harm or kill a depersonalized symbol than a fellow human being.

Effective survival means changing that depersonalized role the hostage has been forced into and emerging as a human being in the eyes of the terrorists. The key element in this change is communication. That means talking, of course, but it also means listening, moving, gesturing, smiling, nodding, and engaging in other behaviors that can begin to establish a connection with the terrorists and show one's essential humanness. These types of communication can build a rapport between terrorists and hostages so that the polarities separating them can appear, for a time at least, to be reduced. When a hostage talks with the terrorists about his or her personal life, interests, family, work, sports, or life at home, the personal individuality of the hostage begins to emerge. Listening to, but not supporting, the terrorists' views about their concerns and their cause helps the hostage to bridge the gap and build an essential connection. Mutual distrust, fear, hate, and suspicion wane as this connection develops so that terrorists and hostage may become more sympathetic to each other. This rapport or mutual accord makes it much less likely that the terrorists will be able, psychologically, to hurt or kill the hostage.

The role played by the hostage during this stage is more complex and difficult than that during the intimidation stage. He or she can be more assertive, but not aggressive; passive, but not submissive; cooperative, but not collaborative; respectful, but not obsequious. The hostage can express personal values and beliefs but should not argue and attempt to force them on the terrorists. The hostage can listen to the views of the terrorists politely and with interest but not slavishly. Nor should the hostage ever pander to their views or cause; the terrorists will quickly detect this type of insincerity.

A delicate balance must be maintained here, and the hostage must be ever alert to overstepping narrow boundaries. As the connection develops, the hostage can test the limits of it just as a child might with parents. The parent-child relationship is analogous to that of terrorist-hostage as it relates to the person with the ultimate power and control. A hostage who is uncomfortable with this enforced role will have more trouble coping with the situation and will tend to react too aggressively (in a futile effort to reassert adult control) or too submissively (as a result of being regressed to a childlike state out of fear). The hostage should work toward establishing and maintaining communication and rapport—the keys to survival. This is especially important when these efforts accomplish a reduction in symbolizing and depersonalization.

The Stockholm Syndrome

Named for the Swedish city in which a robber and his hostages developed an intense, personal, and reciprocal relationship during their several days together in a bank vault, this psychological process is much talked about but little understood. Not all unusual interactions between terrorists and hostages can be attributed to this syndrome, nor does it explain all the seemingly strange behavior that can occur during the ordeal of a hostage situation. If a hostage can bring about the development of the Stockholm syndrome, by playing proper roles during specific stages, however, it can mean the difference between death and survival. This process, which took place with at least one of his captors, was instrumental in saving the life of U.S. Army Brig. Gen. James Dozier during his kidnapping by the Italian Red Brigades in December 1981 (see the "hit list" in the Introduction).

Three essential factors determine the establishment of the Stockholm syndrome. First, minimal violence has been directed at a hostage by the terrorists. If the terrorists are continually aggressive and brutal, there is little hope of any sort of positive relationship developing.

Second, *mutual* liking, interest, understanding, and respect develop between a hostage and terrorist. This, of course, is what the hostage is deliberately working toward in his or her communication efforts with the terrorists.

Third, the hostage experiences an increasing distrust and fear of the authorities (police, military, special weapons and tactics [SWAT] team, government officials) outside the hostage situation. This paranoia results from a growing identification with the terrorists so that the hostage "catches" their anxiety about those outside. Former hostages often state that they feared a rescue strike more than violence from the terrorists. Hostages are aware that rescue strikes can produce numerous casualties. This occurred when Egyptian commandos stormed an EgyptAir flight that had been hijacked to Malta in November 1985. Nearly sixty passengers died in the confusion and fire that resulted from this badly executed rescue attempt. These fears of hostages and their sense of common fate with the terrorists draw the two groups even closer together.

The Stockholm syndrome reverses psychological ties and emotional reactions from what they normally are for people; it is often quite confusing to hostages after the incident is over. The cost of the Stockholm syndrome is a certain amount of distress and conflict; but the benefit is a greatly enhanced chance for survival.

General Dozier used the Stockholm syndrome to survive successfully his kidnapping and threatened death for alleged war crimes by the Red Brigades, a revolutionary terrorist group in Italy.[5] Before he was kidnapped, General Dozier lived with his wife in the penthouse of a secured apartment building in Verona. He was surveilled for six weeks by the Red Brigades. His wife noticed the surveillance and reported it to him, but he ignored her warning. The Red Brigades, disguised as plumbers, entered the building ostensibly to fix a leaking washing machine in the Doziers' utility room. His wife was suspicious and asked the general not to let them into their apartment, but he did anyway. After a scuffle, the terrorists chained Mrs. Dozier in the utility room and took General Dozier out in a box. Mrs. Dozier banged on the pipes for several hours to attract attention. The Italian Caribinieri (federal police), assisted by the American FBI, launched a massive manhunt.

During his captivity, General Dozier was moved to several safe houses and was kept hooded and manacled. Finally, the terrorists settled on a second-floor apartment in Padua above a grocery store. He was kept in a room inside a partitioned tent. His guard sat on one side of the partition with an alarm button on his chair and a locked and loaded weapon in his hand. He had strict orders to kill the general if anything went wrong.

On his side of the partition, General Dozier was manacled to a cot. He was forced to wear headphones and listen to rock and roll music. Terrorists know about the Stockholm syndrome, too, and try to prevent communication.

General Dozier, fully realizing the danger he was in, made every effort to communicate. He discussed his manacles with the terrorists, and the terrorists moved them so he could be more comfortable. He also talked about the music they were playing, and they changed it to something he could tolerate. He discussed the food, which was too rich and causing him to gain weight. They talked about their families. He listened to their cause and grievances. He played cards with his guards, who were as bored as he was.

After about six weeks, the Caribinieri determined where the Red Brigades were holding General Dozier. He was asleep and manacled to his cot when they mounted their rescue strike. Launching a grandstand assault, the Caribinieri alerted the terrorists in the process, but the general's guard dropped his gun without firing a shot.

The guard had been given strict orders. He had a weapon, knew how to use it, and had time to kill General Dozier. During his interrogation at police headquarters, he was asked why he did not kill the general. His answer is a basic example of the lifesaving effect of the Stockholm syndrome in action: "I no longer saw the enemy. I just saw a sleeping man." It may be difficult to communicate with feared and hated captors, but a hostage should make every effort. Communication can be lifesaving, and the Stockholm syndrome can enable the hostage to survive with honor.

It is necessary for the hostage to make repeated attempts to communicate with the captors. Communication and rapport are the keys to survival. Establishing communication can reduce depersonalization of the hostage, assist in getting health and welfare needs met, develop rapport that may lead to respect, and foster development of the Stockholm syndrome. A hostage has specific roles to play at each stage at captivity, just as the captors have their roles. Effectively playing the roles of captive can have lifesaving consequences. The captive must be in emotional control as much as possible, be self-disciplined and respectful, and not be discouraged when communication attempts are thwarted. The captive must walk a narrow path between overcompliance on one side and excessive resistance or challenges to the captors' authority on the other. The middle phase of captivity, when a custodial routine has been established, is the best time to work on communication and rapport. The development of a positive relationship between captor and captive (the Stockholm syndrome) is a mutual process.

THE RESOLUTION STAGE

A hostage-taking incident can be resolved by one or two methods—negotiation or liberation. If resolution occurs through negotiation, the custodial stage may fade almost imperceptibly into the resolution phase. In resolution by liberation, the change from the custodial stage to resolution is abrupt and unexpected because the rescue team always makes a sudden strike to surprise both terrorists and hostages. Obviously, emotions and roles differ, depending on how the episode is resolved.

Resolution by Negotiation

The popularity of exciting rescue scenarios on television often give the impression that hostages are usually freed through liberation, but the vast majority of hostage-taking situations are resolved by negotiation. This method certainly is not as dramatic or thrilling, but it is a great deal safer.

Emotions

The hostages may have no indication that the episode is moving toward resolution, but they may become intent on the smallest scraps of information that could support (or dash) their hopes that captivity will soon be over. Consequently, they become vulnerable to emotional ups and downs that can be quite painful. If the situation seems to be resolving, hopes will slowly rise, along with the fear of disappointment. This stage is characterized by fluctuating hopes, rumors that evoke strong feelings of either encouragement or despair, extreme efforts at optimism as the hostages look for signs that they will soon be freed, periodic fears that more violence will erupt, discouragement when hopes collapse, and frustration and anger at those outside who seem to be doing nothing to resolve the situation. When the hostages are finally moved toward freedom and reunion with friends and family, they often feel a mixture of relief, suppressed joy, and fear that at the last minute something will go wrong. Even after being reunited and returning home to friends and family, some hostages report a lingering shadow of this final fear.

Roles

Roles, like emotions, are dictated by the manner in which the incident is resolved. If this occurs through negotiation, the hostage's role is little different from that during the custodial phase. It is one of self-control and self-containment; the hostage provides support to fellow hostages and maintains communications and rapport with the terrorists. This last is especially important. As the situation moves toward a negotiated conclusion, the terrorists are likely to become tense, anxious, and potentially violent again. They, too, fear that something will go wrong with their plans, such as a last-minute tactical strike.

Resolution by Liberation

In this scenario, the relative boredom and doldrums of the typical custodial stage are suddenly and violently sundered as the tactical strike rescue team comes through the doors, literally with guns blazing. We have all watched it on television with feelings of excitement and amazement. "Busting" terrorists with SWAT strikes gets big play in Hollywood.

Emotions

The genuine article, especially when one is in the middle of it and the bullets and bombs are real, is quite different. Fear, confusion, excitement, and terror are likely to skyrocket and be wildly mixed. The hostages may return to the intense panic and frozen fright of the intimidation stage, or they may feel almost nothing as their denial defenses lock out any immediate experience of emotion. Time distortion may again occur, with the rescue scenario unfolding in slow motion. This stage will be mercifully brief, however, as the tactical team quickly takes control of the situation.

The hostages must still maintain emotional control during and after the rescue operation and not expect the tactical team to welcome them back with open arms. This can be difficult for those who feel their ordeal is suddenly over now that "the cavalry has arrived." The hostages must expect the rescue team to be firm, even rough, until a positive identification of each person has been made. A cautious approach is prudent and necessary because terrorists have feigned death or pretended to be hostages after a rescue operation in order to escape or to strike back at the tactical team or the hostages.

51

Roles

During the liberation, role behavior of the hostages should be much like that during the initial intimidation stage—outward compliance and a low profile. A tactical hostage rescue is a rapid-fire, explosive event.

Most rescue teams use the so-called "Israeli style." Doors are blown. Thunder-flash (stun) grenades temporarily blind and deafen everyone. The team charges in with guns blazing, shouting, "Everybody down! Get down! Get down!" The rescuers have only moments to secure the situation and rescue the hostages—they shoot first and ask questions later. Compliance is especially important at this point. Most teams are trained to fire instantly at *anyone* showing weapons or any aggressive movement.

Hostage survival in a rescue operation is a matter of self-control and a very low profile. The hostage's role is the same as it was during the initial stage of captivity: get down, stay low, blend with the group, and comply with instructions of the rescue team. Because the team cannot immediately tell the difference between the good guys and the bad guys, the hostages should expect firm, aggressive control until identities have been confirmed. They should make no attempt to assist the rescue team with its mission and *never* pick up a fallen weapon. Any movement should be made slowly and only on orders from a team member.

These survival instructions for hostages during a rescue attempt are particularly important. Most hostages survive the ordeal and return home alive and well; but a RAND Corporation study of 77 hostage situations found that more than 70 percent of hostage deaths occurred during rescue operations.[6] This figure alone demonstrates the vital importance of complying with the instructions.

Table 1 summarizes the three stages of a hostage crisis, the terrorists' goals at each stage, and the appropriate role behavior of hostages that is specific to each stage. These practices and procedures have been found lifesaving in a large number of hostage-taking incidents over time. If you should ever have the misfortune to find yourself in such a situation, apply them to improve your chances for survival.

SPECIAL CONSIDERATIONS

Two final and opposite aspects of hostage-taking must be considered: (1) "suicide by terrorist" and (2) constraints on terrorist violence.

Suicide by Terrorist

Occasionally, hostages behave in such a way as to invite death from the terrorists. Although this type of apparent suicide may seem bizarre, it can occur out of rage, frustration, and exhaustion. A group of hostages may have to deal with the irrational acts of one of them because such behavior is a threat to all.

The most well-known instance of "suicide by terrorist" occurred in April 1980 during the Iraqi hostage-barricade incident at the Iranian embassy in Princess Gate, London. Throughout the week-long negotiations, one Iranian hostage constantly provoked, baited, argued with, and belittled the

TABLE 1. Three Stages of a Hostage Crisis

Stages	Terrorist Goals	Hostage Roles
Intimidation	Control	Comply with terrorist demands
Custodial	Negotiation	Communication with terrorists
	Demands	Establish rapport
	Publicity	Develop the Stockholm syndrome
Resolution	Survival	
Negotiation		Maintain self-control, be calm
Liberation		Get down, stay low, blend with group
		Do not try to help rescue team
		Expect firm control
		Comply with rescue team instructions

Iraqi terrorists. The hostage argued points of Islamic law and interpretations of the Koran with the Iraqis in a demeaning and derogatory manner. Other hostages tried to quiet him and pointed out the danger in which he placed all of them. Toward the end of the week, as the terrorists saw their cause failing, they shot this provocative hostage. His death precipitated a rescue strike by the British SAS counterterrorism team. All of the terrorists but one were subsequently killed. This rare phenomenon of suicide by terrorist, dubbed the London syndrome, appears to be the psychological opposite of the Stockholm syndrome.

Constraints on terrorist violence

Important psychological and practical constraints on the violence of the terrorists' behavior are present during a hostage-taking episode. The terrorists have taken hostages to obtain public attention and political leverage. If they are too brutal in their behavior toward the hostages, they may lose support from the public to whom they are trying to appeal, thus hurting their cause.

54

Terrorists know that taking hostages is a risky business; they are vulnerable during and after a hostage-taking. Terrorists have been killed in tactical rescue strikes, as they were at Mogadishu and Entebbe. They have been captured following incidents, such as the TWA flight 847 and the *Achille Lauro* hijackings. If they are bent purely on revenge killing and destruction, they can use methods that are safer for themselves, as they did in the 1986 La Belle Disco bombing in Berlin (see the "hit list" in the Introduction).

That a group of terrorists has gone to the trouble and risk *to themselves* of taking hostages at all is an indication that they have a vested interest in preserving the hostages' lives. This does not mean that the terrorists are especially humane under their angry rhetoric; it is simply good business. Terrorists do not achieve lengthy public and media attention by wanton, senseless killing of their hostages. Statistically speaking, most hostages survive.

In 1985, Brian Jenkins commented, and it is largely true today, "Simply killing a lot of people has seldom been a terrorist objective. Terrorists want a lot of people *watching*, not a lot of people *dead*. . . . Statistics bear this out. Only 15 to 20 percent of all terrorist incidents involve fatalities; and of those, two-thirds involve only one death. Less than 1 percent of the thousands of terrorist incidents that have occurred in the last two decades involve 10 or more fatalities; incidents of mass murder are truly rare."[7] This statement remains largely true today. Brutal and heinous incidents, such as the bombing of Pan Am flight 103 over Lockerbie,

Scotland, in December 1988, which killed 259 passengers and 11 people on the ground, actually occur *infrequently*.

The issues of constraints on terrorist violence and how violence may be predicted from the terrorists' motives are further discussed in Chapter 6.

55

CHAPTER 4

Coping with Captivity

Following the discussion of behaviors a captive should engage in and the roles to play to improve survival chances during the three stages of a hostage-taking episode in Chapter 3, it is helpful to describe some of the psychological problems and dilemmas that arise for individuals and groups in captivity.

Although most hostage-taking episodes are over within days to weeks, some hostages have been held much longer. These include hostages held by Iran for 444 days (November 1979 to January 1981) and the Americans held captive in Lebanon—several for longer than six years. Of course, some of the Vietnam POWs displayed amazing ability to withstand the stress of captivity and survive with honor and integrity for longer than eight arduous years.

Long-term captivity presents major challenges to the sanity, health, and survival of the victim, but psychologists have learned much, especially from the experiences of the Vietnam POWs, about what people can do to survive these lengthy and painful ordeals. In addition to the psychological stages through which one progresses in adapting to long-term captivity, this chapter reviews the stages of recovery following release and repatriation. Individual and group problems that occur during long-term captivity are also examined. The emotional aftermath of a hostage-taking for both victims and their families is considered. Former captives have used many coping skills and techniques to survive. These methods can be effectively applied by any captive or hostage regardless of circumstances or length of incarceration. A detailed, practical description of these methods is given in the final section.

Behavioral scientists now understand more about the nature of captivity and how to cope with it effectively than ever before. Psychologists and psychiatrists have had ample opportunities in recent years to evaluate captives who have survived and to learn about the factors that helped them to cope during and after captivity. This information should reassure those who feel that the captivity experience would be so unique and terrible they would not survive it. There are no superheroes in captivity. Most former hostages and POWs who struggled through captivity are ordinary people. They coped as best they could and survived with honor, but many did not believe at the time that they would or could survive. Most people are amazed to discover what they are truly made of when the chips are down.

Former Navy psychiatrist Richard Rahe has studied captivity stress and psychological reactions in the Vietnam POWs, the Iranian hostages, and those aboard TWA flight 847, as well as individual kidnap victims. Dr. Rahe, in collaboration with Ellen Genender, has summarized his research findings in a model that describes stages of adaptation to and recovery from captivity stress.[1] This model has a nice symmetry to it with six stages each as one enters and then, later, leaves captivity. In presenting his model, I have augmented it with findings from other researchers experienced in the field. The times given in each stage are approximate.

STAGES OF ADJUSTMENT TO CAPTIVITY

The six stages of adjustment are based on psychological reactions to becoming a prisoner. Most captivity sequences begin abruptly, even violently. The hijacking of TWA flight 847 began with the hijackers jumping up, waving weapons, running down the aisle, and screaming, "We come to die! We come to die!"

Startle/Panic—Seconds to Minutes

In the first stage, victims immediately feel intensely fearful, defenseless, confused, and in a state of panic, which can lead to "frozen fright."[2] Victims may also experience tunnel vision, poor memory of these events later, and time distortion in which everything appears to move in slow motion. In a cockpit emergency, for example, time distortion can be especially dangerous because the situation often deteriorates at a rate faster than the pilot perceives it.[3] Pilots, of course, are thoroughly trained to counter the effects of panic. They do not have time to think rationally and must react automatically in an emergency situation.

The best courses of action are either to act automatically *if you are required to take action and have been trained* (a pilot has to deal with an engine flame-out, for example), or not to act at all until you have calmed down, sized up the situation, and developed a plan (a passenger in a terrorist hijacking should follow the latter course).

Reactions in these early moments are familiar as Selye's general arousal or fight-flight reaction.[4] Maximum physical ability is quickly reached through the complex physiology and psychology of this reaction. Great strength and endurance result, but thinking, judgement, decision making, and other higher mental functions are temporarily limited. The combination of being physically stimulated but mentally impaired can be literally deadly during a hostage-taking, hijacking, bank robbery, combat, or any sudden and highly stressful situation. *Don't act unless you must act* can be a lifesaving rule.

59

Coping strategies: Rely on past emergency training, self-discipline, and the instant calm breath method (ICBM). The later section on stress reduction methods and coping strategies gives detailed instructions for applying these techniques.

Disbelief—Minutes to Hours

Startle and panic fade rapidly and give way to denial and numbing in the second stage. Hostages feel a sense of disbelief: "This can't be happening to me" or "This is a nightmare and I'll soon waken." They often have hopes for immediate rescue or massive retaliation and feel that the authorities will not let the situation continue. Later, disappointment when the authorities apparently have not intervened gives rise to a sense of the failed protector described by Martin Symonds[5] and discussed later in this chapter.

In a hostage-taking episode, violence and beatings can take place as the terrorists rapidly try to establish their control during the intimidation stage. POWs have been tortured, threatened with death, and killed for perishable tactical information or "confessions" of war crimes during this stage.

Coping strategies: Use talk down, observer reaction, and ICBM.

Hypervigilance—Hours to Days

Because of the emotional numbing of the previous stage, hostages may have few feelings, but they become extremely wary, acutely vigilant, and attentive to small details during the third stage.

Hypervigilance is a valuable coping technique. By studying the captors, you can gain some control of the situation. If you are released by negotiation or make a successful escape, memorize the captors' locations, appearances, habits, weapons, and the like. You can provide useful intelligence for a rescue operation or negotiations for any remaining hostages. Try to obtain an orientation to the passage of time and your location, even if you are blindfolded or hooded. Familiarity makes captivity more bearable.

Resistance/Compliance—Days to Weeks

During this fourth stage, the captors will attempt to make you comply by giving information for exploitation and propaganda purposes. Your challenge is to develop a more sophisticated and flexible resistance posture. You may be incarcerated for an indefinite time. How do you choose your best approach? Effective resistance to the captors' efforts at exploitation is a matter of testing both your own and the captors' limits.

Coping strategies: Physical fitness activities, communication with other captives, faith, prayer, and thoughts of home and loved ones.

Depression—Weeks to Months

Isolation or solitary confinement is especially difficult at the critical fifth stage because of the loss of your freedom, possibly your future, your contact with loved ones, and everything you value in life. Usually, there is limited contact with others, including guards.

Watch for signs of depression and despair in yourself and others; the signs are vitally important. POWs refer to this stage as "hitting the bottom." They all went through it to a greater or lesser extent. Psychologically, it was necessary in order for them to fully accept their captivity. Symptoms of serious depression include excessive sleep, loss of appetite, lethargy, poor self-care or hygiene, avoidance of communication, weight loss, and rejection of food and water. POWs felt overwhelmed by helplessness, hopelessness, guilt for their performance during interrogations, and suicidal thoughts, although there have been few documented suicides in captivity.

Coping strategies: Communication with other captives is especially important for support, morale, and maintaining a rational perspective. Other valuable methods are keeping your mind active with creative mental work, life planning, fantasy, imagination, and a good sense of humor.

Gradual Acceptance—Months to Years

During the final stage of adjustment, you begin to realize and accept that rescue is not imminent, so you start living from day to day. Small things take on great importance. You may take hours to clean the cell or make friends with the bugs and creatures that inhabit it. Make daily activities, such as eating, exercise, and toilet functions into "events" to pass time. Read or write, if permitted. Establish and stick to a schedule of daily routines to combat boredom and loneliness and the despair that can result. The passage of time becomes distorted—days are long, but months fly by. Mental activities and communication with others are even more important for coping.

STAGES OF RECOVERY FROM CAPTIVITY

The six stages of recovery reflect psychological reactions to repatriation. All captives live for rescue, release, and repatriation with their country, home, and loved ones. Few realize that their ordeal is *not* over when they are free. The trauma of any captivity, long or short, takes a period of adjustment when they return to freedom. Captives need time to heal their psychological and physical wounds; they need time for recovery.

Brief Euphoria—Seconds to Minutes

Captives often feel a deep mistrust that release is just another false hope. Repatriation may bring only fleeting feelings of happiness during the initial stage. Efforts to appear joyful in order to meet others' expectations can be difficult. Welcome home celebrations can fall flat.

Hyperarousal—Minutes to Hours

At this second stage, former captives are often overstimulated and mentally slowed. They may feel punch-drunk. This feeling can be complicated by sleep deprivation during extensive travel to return home.

Compliance/Resistance—Hours to Days

Captives become accustomed to complying with orders from guards and others. During the third stage, they may overextend themselves to meet the demands of family, press, wellwishers, and doctors. Soon after their release, they break routines, appointments, and limits. Although this can be frustrating to the medical staff that is trying to evaluate them, it is generally a good sign of progress toward normalcy as the former captives realize they do not have to comply with all of these demands.

Denial—Days to Weeks

When first released, former captives admit to problems resulting from the ordeal. During this fourth stage, however, they announce: "Everything is OK!" or "The doctors worry too much!" They usually have considerable need for continuing medical and psychological care. Denying the existence of problems caused by captivity does not make them disappear and can cause serious long-term difficulties.

Because captives have been deprived, they may impulsively overindulge after they have been freed. Depending on their judgment, some impulsive behaviors and long-range decisions need to be monitored and possibly curbed. Family members can be helpful in restoring balance and maintaining perspective.

63

Restitution—Weeks to Months

Former captives may not be prudent and moderate following the deprivations of incarceration. Family members should be cautious of their excessive self-indulgence, for example, in food (and resulting obesity), impulsive spending, or investments that are not carefully considered. During this fifth stage, particularly, they may be influenced by unscrupulous persons who present schemes to capitalize on their experiences and offer riches and fame. Former captives can be quite vulnerable to these scams.

They may have experienced dulling of their emotional and mental functions during captivity so that they have difficulty communicating with family and friends. Former captives need to be cautious about overeagerness to return to work; adjustments and retraining may be necessary. Repeated recitals of their experiences seem to be therapeutic. Lecturing, writing, or retelling events to family, friends, and others can be helpful.

Gradual Readjustment—Months to Years

The psychological trauma caused by captivity can range from mild to severe. Recovery is slow, painful, and difficult; some former captives never fully recover. Dr. Rahe has compared recovery rates during this final stage for different captive groups. Life-long anxiety and depression can affect individuals who suffer severe and prolonged captivity stress, such as concentration camp survivors. World War II POWs from the Pacific theater and Korean POWs had a 25- to 30-year recovery period for physical and mental illnesses. In contrast, the Vietnam POWs had only an 8- to 10-year recovery period, which Dr. Rahe attributes in part to the effectiveness of captivity survival training instituted by the military after the Korean War.[6] The Boy Scouts are right—being prepared helps.

PSYCHOLOGICAL PROBLEMS OF INDIVIDUAL CAPTIVES

The powerful states of emotional arousal caused by the fight-flight reaction during a hostage-taking episode can cause considerable psychological upheaval for the unaware captive. The main problems of individual captivity, especially when the hostage is kept in isolation, are fear and anxiety on the one hand and boredom and despair on the other. These emotions can lead to other psychological difficulties that should be combated with effective coping methods such as those described in the later section on stress reduction methods and coping strategies.

Fear and Anxiety

These universal initial reactions recur throughout captivity and can last for quite awhile after the captive has been rescued or released. During captivity, fear of the unknown results from the unpredictability of the captors' behavior. Fear can result in action paralysis; inappropriate reactions, such as uncontrolled laughter; and impulsive acts, including thoughtless escape attempts and attacks against the captors. Fear and anxiety can be moderated and controlled through various stress reduction techniques, as described in the later section.

Boredom and Despair

The two worst psychological problems of long-term captives, especially those confined in isolation, are boredom and despair. By too much thinking about the difficulties of the situation, a captive can let his or her imagination become an enemy that leads to excessive, nonproductive worry and dwells on catastrophic outcomes. Severe depression can result. At its worst, depression can lead to totally withdrawing, refusing food and drink, avoiding communication, lying unresponsively in a fetal position, and succumbing to a type of suicide known as willed death or "give-up-itis," as it was called by Korean POWs. The best coping methods for dealing with these feelings include physical fitness, mental activities, faith, prayer, thoughts of loved ones, future life plans, fantasy, and daily structuring of time and events.

Guilt

Guilt comes from feelings of failure: "What did I do wrong to get myself captured?" Guilt is based on the irrational belief that being held hostage is somehow a punishment for wrongdoing or failure. False and exaggerated expectations of heroism to which the captive has not measured up, known popularly as the John Wayne syndrome, can produce guilt. Feelings of guilt generally mean that the hostage has confused pride with honor and needs to rethink this perspective. Guilt can produce self-recrimination, negativism, and depression.

Fatalism

The negative and nihilistic belief that all will turn out for the worst can cause self-fulfilling prophecies. As a result, captives unwittingly tend to act in ways that make adverse events happen. They are not usually aware that their attitudes are affecting events around them. Rather, they use the occurrence of such events as proof that the fatalistic attitude is an accurate assessment of their situation. Such an airtight belief system, especially in a captivity environment, can be convincing, compelling, and eventually self-destructive. To counter this, a positive mental attitude and careful evaluation of beliefs and perceptions are vital.

Pain

Pain can result from a high stress load, and it is usually psychosomatic unless there is actual injury. Psychosomatic pain is quite real and often takes the form of severe headaches, chest or back pain, or nausea and stomach pain. Numbness or tingling in the extremities sometimes occurs. If there is no injury or medical condition causing the pain, it should be regarded by the captive as a sign of stress and the need to employ any of the stress reduction methods. Hypnosis can be particularly helpful and effective. Pain often abates or disappears when the stress level has been lowered.

Psychiatric Symptoms

An overwhelming fear that one is going crazy, severe depression, and auditory and visual hallucinations have been experienced by captives in long-term isolation. These feelings and hallucinations have been artificially produced in the laboratory in sensory deprivation experiments. Usually transient products of isolation, they are harmless in normal people and will disappear as adjustment to captivity improves. Actually, hallucinations can be rather entertaining during isolation if they are accepted as normal under the circumstances and are not feared. Contact and communication with others can help any "craziness" to abate, as can better contact with reality through mental and physical activities and efforts to structure time and events.

Beliefs have a profound effect on a captive and can make the difference between life and death. Knowing that others have been in similar, or even worse, situations and have returned alive can be a powerful impetus to a captive's belief in his or her own survival. Belief in self, in country, and in God are primary sources of strength for many long-term captives. Many of them report greatly increased confidence, faith, and surety in themselves, and a deepening of their religious values.

67

PSYCHOLOGICAL PROBLEMS FOUND IN GROUP CAPTIVITY

When people are held captive as a group, another set of problems, as well as new opportunities, arise. The personality of each individual affects others. The development of group dynamics can make life difficult for all of the captives, or new supports and strengths can result that help everyone to deal better with the stress of captivity. Knowing what difficulties to expect in a group captivity environment, how the captors might exploit these problems, and how to cope with them can help immeasurably toward enhancing the group's survival.

Captives in a group situation are often more critical of others' behavior than of their own. This common tendency can lead to lack of trust, paranoia, group divisiveness, and mutual suspicion, and it is certainly one that experienced captors try to exploit. Captors use divide-and-conquer tactics to capitalize on this tendency in order to manipulate the group or individual hostages. They try to elicit excessive compliance by playing the captives off against each other in order to obtain information, induce cooperation and collaboration, and exploit the group for propaganda purposes. Because the main goals of political terrorists are propaganda and publicity for their cause, both civilian and military hostages need to be on guard.

The captives should keep faith with each other and suspend judgments until they are freed. Such efforts are especially important for group morale and enable captives to resist their captors' manipulations. Communication and sharing of information are crucial. Message drops, the tap code (quadratic alphabet), and other signals can be used if direct conversation between captives is prohibited. Communication with each other is the single most significant factor in a group POW or hostage situation. It helps to maintain morale, avoids divide-and-conquer tactics, reduces confusion, and gives needed psychological support. Isolation or prohibitions against talking require the captives to find novel means of communication. The tap code was widely used by Vietnam POWs to communicate with each other. They not only tapped, but whistled, coughed, swept (and, as recounted by some POWs, even belched and farted!) the code for communication and contact. It is that vital!

Signs of Stress in Captives

Stress overload can result in hysterical or impulsive behavior that is a danger not only to the individual hostage but to everyone. Signs of stress include withdrawal, depression, and unwillingness to communicate or, at the other extreme, excessive emotionality, agitation, provocativeness, and threatening behaviors. In addition, excessive suspicion, grandiose plans, and emotional euphoria are extremely serious signs because they may presage impulsive, "heroic" acts against the terrorists that could have serious consequences for the group. These stress overload reactions are comparable to the John Wayne and the London syndromes; they are all highly dangerous and potentially suicidal.

The other captives should attempt to calm a person under stress overload and help that individual to regain control. This is important to everyone's welfare. People tend to be overly responsive in high-stress circumstances so that even minor actions, such as a calming word or two, a smile, a touch, or thumbs-up, can be quite reassuring. Sudden and precipitate actions on the part of the captives must be avoided, especially at the beginning and near the end of an episode when the captors themselves are most tense, excitable, and prone to quick violence.

Signs of Stress in Hostage-Takers

The captors also should be observed for signs of stress similar to those experienced by the captives. These signs may signal a violent outburst toward the captives. This is a difficult situation to deal with and must be defused as soon as possible. Development of the Stockholm syndrome between some of the hostages and captors can greatly help. Uli Derickson's relationship with the two hijackers aboard TWA flight 847 enabled her to defuse many potentially dangerous and possibly deadly situations throughout that protracted episode. The captives should attempt to distract a captor who is showing signs of stress by a question or request or through direct intervention. Conveying a sense of calmness may also help to reduce tensions. Individual captives should be cautious in their efforts at intervention, however, because they could direct the captor's violence toward themselves.

EMOTIONAL AFTERMATH

70

Much detailed understanding of the emotional aftermath following severe and stressful events is built on psychological research with victims of trauma. Whether these are victims of rapes, muggings, kidnappings, hostage-takings, assassination attempts, or natural or man-made disasters or the like, the healing process is much the same. Like any healing process, it can have its difficulties. Complications can set in; the healing may be slow and difficult. Because of advances in psychological understanding of the healing process, however, professional consultation can make an important difference when difficulties occur.

All captives look forward to release or rescue as the end of their trouble, fear, and pain. Because they have been under great stress, sometimes for considerable periods, both the mind and the body need time to heal. Definite stages and reaction patterns are present during this process. When former captives do not understand what they are going through or its healing purpose, they often find their reactions disturbing. Knowledge that these reactions are part of a natural and normal healing process can be immeasurably reassuring.

A captive's recovery generally follows the order described above in the section on the stages of recovery. Most former captives pass through these stages.[7] However, it should be remembered that all individuals have their own private experiences and backgrounds. Each person's adjustment after captivity may be different. Also, these patterns and sequences are not firm and fixed. The former captive should regard them as cycles, within which one moves back and forth.

The Emotional Turmoil of Healing

A mixture of *shock, disbelief* and *denial* may be the first reaction after release. At first, former hostages are unable to accept the fact that the ordeal is over. Some may be psychologically numb. Others may show evidence of continuation of the Stockholm syndrome, which indicates poor reality contact. Relief and brief euphoria may precede or follow the shock phase. These reactions are often short-lived because of fatigue.

In the *hyperarousal stage* that follows, the combination of overstimulation and exhaustion (some captives have compared it with honeymoon sex) makes the individual feel agitated, edgy, nervous, and fidgety despite the extreme fatigue. Sleep and appetite routines are often disturbed. The former hostage may experience insomnia or want to sleep most of the time (hypersomnia). Nightmares are common. Food may be uninteresting or repugnant.

Depression may set in for a time. The individual may have a sense of insecurity, excessive fear, vulnerablility, and anger against the authorities. Many people going through these reactions describe themselves as feeling different from those who have not had a similar experience.

The captives' *sense of the failed protector,* or abandonment by the authorities, may result in feelings of anger and outrage. These feelings result from the belief that the authorities did not fulfill their responsibilities to keep the individual safe from harm by providing adequate security to prevent the hostage-taking or by rapidly intervening to end it. Feelings of abandonment and anger at the failed protector can result from childlike expectations that parents and other authority figures should provide all-around protection from life's harms and dangers.[8] Persistence of these feelings indicates professional help may be needed to work through the reactions.

Mood swings are common. Emotions may go through intense cycles of ups and downs. Thoughts and feelings about the events of captivity intrude into consciousness unexpectedly and at unwanted times. Victims sometimes want to talk repeatedly and in detail about their experiences; at other times, they want no reminder of them. At first, these ambivalent reactions are intense and frequent, but they slowly decline. Writing books or lecturing about their experiences may be therapeutic. Family and friends are advised to follow the desires of the victim in talking or not talking about the captivity. They should expect no timetable for the former hostage to finish discussing these experiences.

Anger underlies a victim's feelings of depression. It is a good indicator of recovery, although it may be difficult for family and friends. The victim often asks, "Why me?" in a rhetorical, demanding way. There is no acceptable answer to this question because it often comes from a mixture of rage, guilt, and self-pity. Expression of the anger and other feelings is part of the psychological healing process and a healthy sign.

As the last of the American hostages held in the Middle East were released in December 1991, the news coverage of this event enabled Americans to witness much of the emotional aftermath and the different temporal stages of readjustment the hostages were going through. Their reactions to captivity varied as a result of the length of time since their release. An article in the 16 December issue of *Time* captured this difference in the postcaptivity feelings of journalist Terry Anderson, who had just been released, and Catholic priest Father Lawrence Jenco, who was freed more than five years ago:

". . . many ex-hostages speak of the need to forgive their former captors. "I'm a Christian and a Catholic," Anderson said last week. "It's required of me that I forgive, no matter how hard it may be." Father Jenco, by contrast, argues, "Anger is a very good emotion. Even Jesus got angry."[9]

Anderson's comment, while laudable, suggests the typical emotional denial and numbing that occur immediately after release. Jenco's remarks indicate movement toward expressing his anger with, perhaps, a bit of *philosophical reflection*, the next stage in this lengthy process during which the question "Why me?" becomes more thoughtful, even spiritual. It contains less anger and demand and assumes a more philosophical tone. The victim attempts to place the event into the context of his or her life and begins to relinquish the pain of past trauma. Intrusive thoughts and emotions are less of a problem. Sleep and appetite generally return to normal. Nightmares may continue, but they are less frequent.

Laying-to-rest is the final phase of healing before the former hostage is able to get on with life. The emotional pain and anguish of the captive experience are gone, although never forgotten. Victims no longer dwell on the events but try to accept them as part of life. Some captives are even able to make their experiences valuable and meaningful and regard them as having fostered growth and constructive development.

Family Reactions

When a family member becomes a POW or hostage, the family goes through stages, emotions, and reactions similar to those of the captive. In a sense, the family is being held hostage, too. It is a stressful ordeal for the family members; their emotional reactions occur both during and after captivity.[10]

The good intentions of families in dealing with former captives after release or rescue can inhibit the recovery process. Some families just want to forget the events and refuse to discuss them. Others may redecorate the house as a way of welcoming the loved one home. If a former captive had been imagining things just as they used to be, this situation can be quite a shock. Some families have an implicit timetable for the end of the former captive's distress and are upset when it is not followed. Open discussion helps greatly.

These recovery stages are similar to the complex reactions that take place during grief. Navigating successfully through these troubled waters is neither simple nor easy. Depending on the victim's psychological constitution, the duration of captivity, and the severity of the stress, recovery may be a difficult process. The victim can "get stuck," be unable to complete working through the recovery process, and join the ranks of the walking wounded. Such emotional scars seriously affect the victim's life and the lives of family members.

Because these stages are complex and difficult for victims and families to deal with, psychological help can be useful. Trained professionals can keep the process on track, reduce the damage of trauma, and support recovery during the aftermath. The sooner victims get help after traumatic events, the better and faster is recovery.

Hostages—Heroes or Martyrs

Winning is important to Americans. Losing face, being humiliated, or feeling powerless can be nearly intolerable. With some notable exceptions, we have had little to feel good about in our encounters with terrorism. We have been made to feel helpless, weak, embarrassed, and humiliated when Americans have been assaulted or taken hostage by a terrorist group or foreign power. When the incident is over, our collective response is to want to undo the damage and feel proud of ourselves and our country once again.

One of the means we have chosen to rid ourselves of our discomfort has been to lionize the former hostages with heroes' welcomes on their return home, ticker-tape parades, meetings with the president, medals and awards, public speaking engagements, and lecture tours. If hostages return alive, we make them heroes; if not, we make them and their families martyrs.

Hostages are neither heroes nor martyrs. They are victims. They and their families have been through a great deal of pain and suffering, much of which has been made public through the aggressive intrusiveness of the media into the private lives of these citizens. Many former hostages report that they are uncomfortable with the public reaction to their return. Making hostages into heroes often distresses them considerably. They do not feel victorious like heroes; they feel like victims who struggled with and survived an ordeal. They do not see themselves as having done anything heroic or deserving of public acclaim and attention any more than the victim of a mugging or rape feels heroic when it is over. They are glad to be back, of course. They are relieved that the ordeal is finally over and that they have survived it.

What the public does not see are the complex psychological reactions and continuing pain that many hostages experience in their efforts to readjust to normal life. Continuing fears, nightmares, daydreams, and flashbacks to incidents that took place during their captivity are common and provoke much anxiety. Personal relationships, sleep, appetite, the ability to concentrate and work, and interest in everyday activities are often disturbed. Thoughts and feelings about their stressful experiences often intrude unbidden into consciousness and cause distress and distraction. Their emotions are frequently unpredictable and labile. They may alternate between a compelling desire to talk endlessly about their

75

experiences and a powerful need to forget them. Reactions of some hostages are so severe as to be diagnosed as post-traumatic stress disorders (PTSD), the same disorder suffered by some Vietnam veterans. In such cases, professional help is essential for complete recovery.

76

The emotional reactions of former hostages are complicated, and in some cases worsened, by the public's need to make them into heroes. Hostages have felt used and abused by their captors. They have firsthand knowledge of how it feels to be pawns in political publicity battles and have felt the pain, anger, and shame of exploitation for alien political purposes. On their return, former hostages may perceive the public's need to make them into heroes as more exploitation. They do not wish to refuse these attentions and aggrandizements of their own countrymen because they know they come with good intentions.

Perhaps in our eagerness to welcome home American hostages and to show our appreciation for what they have suffered, we should be more aware of their needs and the needs of their families. The public's response to their anguish can help to heal the wounds, but trying to make heroes of the former hostages may only increase their conflict. True compassion and understanding are more appropriate for these Americans and their families and certainly in line with our finest traditions.

A society that prizes human rights and freedom will always be vulnerable to terrorist violence. Some of us will become victims. Society has a deeper obligation to the victims than merely to make them heroes when they return. The United States has an important obligation to provide the best care to assist them with readjustment and a return to society. When we give our best, as we did for the Vietnam POWs, the results are positive, healing, and long-lasting. When we ignore our victims, as we largely did for many years with the Vietnam veterans, the results are tragic, destructive, and equally long-lasting. The choice seems simple enough.

STRESS REDUCTION METHODS AND COPING STRATEGIES

This compendium of stress control methods comprises a kit of tools to aid the hostage or POW in controlling adverse emotional reactions and coping with the long-term difficulties of captivity. Many of these procedures are skills that former hostages and POWs have used effectively to aid their survival during captivity.[11] Additional methods have been selected from the vast body of research and practical application in psychological stress management.[12] Most of these tools are valuable in reducing daily life stresses when they are practiced on a routine basis. This provides good preparation for effective use of the methods in a hostage situation.

These stress reduction and coping procedures have been organized into five categories: (1) physical methods, (2) cognitive methods, (3) imaginative methods, (4) mental methods, and (5) belief systems. All of them have been chosen because they work, but they are not magic. Taken together, they can become a powerful set of tools to help victims of terrorism or of any psychological trauma to cope with their ordeals.

Physical Methods

Instantly calm breath method (ICBM): Use active breath control to affect directly the stress (fight-flight) response. Breathe slowly and deeply, exerting positive breath control with emphasis on complete *exhalation* and holding the breath *out* for a few moments before inhaling again. This counters the tendency to hyperventilate when under stress. Add thought stopping and hypervigilance (see below) for a powerful, immediate stress control technique.

78

Physical fitness: Perform physical exercises, such as brisk walking, calisthenics, isometric exercises (flex your muscles against restraints if you are bound), stretching, or yoga. Any type of exercise helps you to stay physically and mentally fit and better able to handle the stress of incarceration.

Progressive muscle relaxation: Visualize muscle groups progressively from toes to head (feet, legs, belly and buttocks, chest and back, arms, neck, and head). Flex each group for a few moments, then relax. Imagine each group relaxing deeply. This method is good for general relaxation and going to sleep, and it is better than counting sheep for treating insomnia.

Autogenic training: Use progressive muscle relaxation but with the added verbal suggestions of warmth and heaviness of the muscles. Both of these exercises begin to induce a mild hypnotic state, which can be helpful for pain reduction.

Biofeedback training: Using a simple electronic (biofeedback) device that monitors the arousal level of the nervous system, you can learn various ways to relax deeply and reduce stress. The monitors are inexpensive and available to the general public, but obviously this method should be learned before you become a captive.

Acupressure: Use finger pressure on acupressure head and body points to relieve tension, headaches, and other stress-related pains and to promote overall relaxation. This method is easily learned but should be studied in advance of captivity. An advantage of acupressure is that you can use it on other persons to help them ease their pain or distress and to feel more relaxed.

Cognitive Methods

Talk down: Your own voice giving reassurance and talking you through a difficult situation can be very calming. Talking out loud is best, but your voice can be effective even if it is only in your mind. Talking yourself down can help change your perceptions of the situation to avoid overreacting.

Observation: The early captivity reaction usually includes emotional numbing with increased sensory acuity (hypervigilance). If you are hooded, for example, your hearing and touch become more sensitive. Use this method to focus your attention, gather information, observe your captors, memorize details, and make mental notes for intelligence purposes. Familiarity makes captivity more bearable by giving you a better sense of control. Your information gathering can be extremely useful to negotiators or tactical teams if you escape or are released through negotiation.

Review of life plans and goals: What better time? There is lots of it. Permit yourself to become more philosophical. Think about your life—what is important and what is not. How would you like to live your life differently when you are released?

Structure of time and events: Maintain a daily schedule and discipline yourself to stick to it. Make the most of simple events, such as eating, going to the toilet, and exercising. Make a calendar or keep a journal, if you can. Do not dwell on an indefinite sentence. Instead, keep a moving time window toward the future; remember, each moment that passes brings the resolution of your captivity that much closer. Live one day at a time.

Imaginative Methods

Directed fantasy: Left on its own, your imagination may tend to focus on the negative possibilities of the captivity situation (catastrophizing). Do not permit that. Use your imagination constructively and positively. Create a vivid, secure, peaceful place in your mind, and dwell there when possible.

Storehouse of memories, knowledge and fantasy: Revisit pleasant memories from the past; create enjoyable fantasies of the future. Relearn by recalling your forgotten knowledge, such as languages, mathematical skills, or names and faces of friends from school.

Mental creativity: Write poetry, music, or stories. Reproduce something meaningful from memory (e.g., Bible verses, Shakespeare's sonnets). Build a house or a boat in your imagination. Play games mentally—checkers, poker, or chess.

Humor: Keep your sense of humor and your sense of the absurd. Make up pet names for your captors. For example, the Iranian hostages called their guards "Farkles," from a popular television comedy show of the time. Try to achieve little victories. Find subtle ways of "getting over" on your captors.

Mental Methods

Thought stopping: Scream a silent "NO!" in your mind to stop depressing and catastrophizing thoughts. Change "channels." Discipline yourself to think about something else whenever thoughts become negative.

Pain control: Called the pain/anxiety spiral, your pain threshold decreases as anxiety increases. Staying calm reduces pain. Because energy follows attention, focusing on pain tends to increase it. Direct your attention away from pain with distraction methods or directed fantasy.

Meditation: Studies have shown that all meditation methods are equally effective in producing the relaxation response and thereby reducing stress. Learn one method well—and use it.

Self-hypnosis: These techniques are easy to learn from the large variety of books and tapes available. Use self-hypnosis for relaxation, calming, pain control, and sleep. Hypnosis can improve memory and fantasy abilities, as well as open channels to unconscious strengths that can be vitally important to a captive.

Belief Systems

Positive mental attitude (PMA): This is one of the best assets any captive can have and is extremely important to maintain.

Beliefs: A person's beliefs have such a fundamental effect on emotion, attitude, and will that they can determine the outcome of a survival situation. Survival often results from believing you will make it. Just as fatalistic beliefs can destroy a captive, PMA and optimistic beliefs can keep you alive through the most adverse circumstances.

Knowledge: Other hostages have been in similar (or worse) situations and survived. This knowledge can be a powerful impetus toward your own survival. Awareness that others have been successful, along with your own positive beliefs, can help you avoid the vicious cycle of loneliness → helplessness → depression → despair.

Religious values, beliefs, and prayer: All of these have inestimable importance to the captive. Most persons who have been held in captivity describe a deepening and enrichment of religious values that greatly aided their survival and sanity. A hostage should not dwell on death, but a philosophy of life or set of religious values that embraces the possibility of death can be literally lifesaving.

Article I of the Code of Conduct for all military members states that military personnel are willing to give their lives in defense of their country and its way of life. I wonder how often and how deeply military personnel really think about what that means. Indeed, there are those times when they are asked to lay it *all* on the line.

Captivity is an ordeal for anyone. For a few, it is the end. For many, it becomes a new beginning.

CHAPTER 5

History and Geopolitics of Terrorism

Modern terrorism has a long history. The goals, objectives, and tactics of terrorists have been much the same over the centuries. Most innovations in modern terrorism comprise technological advances in explosives, communications, weapons, transportation and, most importantly, worldwide media publicity. Little else has changed during the past two thousand years of terrorism. History has important lessons to teach about terrorism—the problems and challenges have been encountered before. As Santayana wrote, "Progress, far from consisting in change, depends on retentiveness. . . . Those who cannot remember the past are condemned to fulfill it."[1]

A large number, perhaps more than three hundred, and a wide diversity of terrorist groups exist in the world today. Yet, in their tactical actions and many of their aims, there are numerous similarities. To impose order on this diversity, both geopolitical and historical approaches are useful and clarifying.

Responses to terrorism by the United States and other countries during the past three decades have consisted largely of crisis management. When a hostage-taking or other incident occurs, much urgency and pressure to resolve it are precipitated. A wiser, more effective approach would consist of policy planning models and response strategies based on historical and geopolitical perspectives that provide insight into the psychologies of the various terrorist groups.

84

MIDDLE EAST

The Zealots and the Sicarii

Terrorism emerged from the cradle of civilization in the Middle East. One of the earliest events that bears most of the hallmarks of a modern terrorist operation took place about 6 B.C. The Jews had been suffering for many years under the oppressive rule of the Roman government. A Jewish revolutionary sect called the Zealots was trying to foment a rebellion, mostly through political action and civil disorder. The action arm of the Zealots was an assassin squad known as the Sicarii, named for the small, curved dagger its members used in their work. Employing a specific "hit list," the Sicarii targeted important, symbolic figures in the Roman government—senators, centurions, judges, and businessmen. These assassinations led to such a resource drain on the government that open warfare eventually erupted, exactly what the Zealots were seeking.[2]

This early terrorist endeavor contains all the elements of modern agitational terrorism: oppressors and oppressed, rebellious group assaulting symbolic targets to create a climate for revolution, and more government repression followed by guerrilla attacks that led to civil war. This same pattern has been successfully followed in many modern countries, especially in Africa and Latin America.[3]

Lex Talionis

Middle Eastern terrorism may be as old as its civilizations. Much of the continual battles and bloodshed in the Middle East over the centuries has been based on the code of Hammurabi. Established by this Babylonian king during the eighteenth century B.C., Hammurabi's code was a set of laws of retributive justice. Its essence was "lex talionis," the Talion principle, proverbially known as "an eye for an eye and a tooth for a tooth." The code of Hammurabi became the foundation for laws and criminal justice in the Middle East, which is why, in some countries, the hand of the thief is amputated in retribution for his crime. Retribution is the basis for the endless family, tribal, and national feuds that have characterized so much of Middle Eastern history. This ancient law of retribution is evident in the ongoing terrorist strikes and counterstrikes between the Palestinians and the Israelis today.

85

The Assassins

Persia of the eleventh century was a center for terrorist activities that were a chilling prelude to their modern counterparts in the Middle East. Hassan al ibn Sabbah, a Shiite cleric and head of a small sect, gathered a group of the faithful around him. Through the deadly and usually suicidal attacks of those terrorists, he initiated a holy war, or *jihad.* These original assassins were the faithful, or *fida'i*—dedicated, suicidal hit men who were willing to die for their holy cause.

Hassan's usual procedure was to place one of his assassins, bearing a knife that the master had personally blessed, into the service of a caliph, vizier, or religious leader whom he wished to influence or assassinate. Sometimes the killer waited for years as he slowly became closer to and gained the trust of his intended target. On Hassan's command, the assassin would spring forth and plunge his dagger into the heart of the victim. Often, these assassins would be killed or kill themselves on the spot. Suicide or death while serving in the jihad, according to fundamentalist Moslem belief, guaranteed the fida'i a special place in heaven.

Hassan established his fortress at Alamat in the mountains north of Tehran. From there, he gained control of Persia, Iraq, Syria, Lebanon, and parts of Turkey. His assassins attacked rival Moslem religious and political leaders, as well as Christian crusaders. Hassan and his successors maintained their power for more than 150 years until 1256, when the Mongol hordes of Ghengis Khan, sweeping through the Middle East, destroyed every civilization and conquered every country in their path.[4]

The Modern Middle East

Most people have the impression that the Middle East is responsible for a great share of anti-American terrorist incidents. In my terrorism classes for military and civilian personnel, students would always rate the Middle East as first in terrorist activity among five major geopolitical regions in the world. Contrary to common perception, the Middle East actually accounts for only about 10 to 11 percent of all worldwide terrorist activity directed against U.S. interests. This figure has remained stable for about ten years, according to U.S. Army statistics from the International Terrorism Assessment Center (ITAC) in Washington, D.C.[5] The psychological effect of these incidents brought about by the ability of Middle Eastern terrorists to command media attention has created the distorted impression of greater frequency of attacks.

To come to grips with the propaganda power of Middle Eastern terrorism, we must understand the psychology of these terrorists, as well as their skill in holding the West hostage to their demands. Consider their holding of American hostages, some for many years, for the primary purpose of trying to manipulate the United States by using human bargaining chips. Americans have great difficulty comprehending those who barter human lives and freedom for political influence or power. Yet, just such hostage-taking and hostage-trading has taken place among families, tribes, and religious and political groups for centuries in the Middle East. Endless blood feuds involving decades of assassination and revenge are not infrequent.

We are dealing with a fundamentalist, fanatical, religious, *and* political mentality in the Middle East. There is no separation of church and state in politics or in individual psychology. Acts of political terrorism are driven by a potentially suicidal religious fervor that gives these people their fanatical character. Moslem fundamentalists continue to believe that self-sacrifice in the name of the jihad will send them straight to heaven. The spirit of Hassan al ibn Sabbah lives on.

The power of this combination of factors results in terrorists who are so dedicated as to be both murderous and suicidal in their battles against the United States. We are seen not only as a political and ideological foe but also as a religious enemy, the great Satan. In the psychology of violent radicalism, ideological motives generally result in attacks on institutions, whereas religious beliefs usually generate attacks against persons. In the Middle East, we must contend with both, often simultaneously. Consider the recent history of anti-American attacks in this area: the American Embassy suicide bombings in Beirut, April 1983 and September 1984; the Marine Corps barracks suicide bombing, October 1983; the murders of Petty Officer Robert Stethem on TWA flight 847, June 1985, and Lt. Col. William Higgins in Beirut, August 1989.

The jihad continues, and we continue to be drawn into it. The fida'i, still willing to die for their cause, use tactics and strategy that are much the same today as they have been for hundreds of years. Suicide bombings are not the isolated acts of deranged madmen. They are typical operations of Moslem guerrilla fighters, who have a different view of life and afterlife than those held in the West. Recognition of how these important cultural and religious differences affect the nature of terrorism and guerrilla operations in the Middle East can have a significant impact on planning, prediction, and counterstrategy.

Profile of Middle Eastern Terrorists

Typically, Middle Eastern terrorists are poorly educated; many are illiterate. They depend on their mullahs and other religious leaders, who attain their positions because of their ability to read the Koran. This gives the mullahs great religious and political power. With little distinction between church and state in the Middle East, political and religious influences govern virtually every act.

Middle Eastern terrorists frequently have state support or sponsorship of their assaults. Their actions are often based on centuries-old blood feuds, attacks against the corruption and evil of religious enemies, or revenge for perceived modern injustices, such as the U.S. support of Israel or the shooting down of an Iranian airliner by the USS *Vincennes*. The United States is seen as the "Great Satan" and the U.S. military as the devil's tool. The targets of these terrorists are mainly persons who are killed for revenge (rather than buildings destroyed for symbolic attack) or kidnapped for extortion and government manipulation. At risk are Americans in general, and U.S. military personnel and Jews in particular. Victims of Middle Eastern terrorists must contend with Mos-

lem fundamentalism mixed with ideological hatred, as those
aboard TWA flight 847 discovered.

A Psychological Autopsy

In June 1985 during the hijacking of TWA flight 847, U.S.
Navy diver Robert Stethem was singled out by the terrorists.
Petty Officer Stethem was readily identifiable. He was not in
uniform, but his youth, short haircut, and physical condition
marked him as a U.S. serviceman. He had no passport; like
the other military men on board the airplane, he was traveling on his military identification card and orders. When the
terrorists learned he and some of the other men were military personnel, they reacted with rage in recalling the shelling of Beirut by the USS *New Jersey* in 1983.

Stethem was a victim of the many facets of terrorism in
the Middle East. He was a scapegoat for the terrorists' hatred
of the United States and the American military, their rage
and fear of what they regarded as evil, and their revenge and
retribution for the shelling of Beirut. There is no indication
that Stethem incurred their wrath by being aggressive or
hostile.[6]

A terrorist told Stethem he *must* die because the terrorist's family had been killed in the shelling. Stethem was sav-
agely beaten and eventually shot. His body was dumped on
the airport tarmac in Beirut. In the terrorists' view, the code
of Hammurabi had been carried out in the spirit of Hassan al
ibn Sabbah—a life for a life. The terrorists' treatment of
Stethem and the other military personnel was also used to
intimidate the rest of the passengers and to assert the terrorists' control.

Perhaps knowledge of the factors unique to Middle Eastern terrorism may help us to understand the brutal bombing
deaths of the Marines in their Beirut barracks and the pas-

sengers and crew of Pan Am flight 103 over Lockerbie, Scotland, as well as the cruel murders of American hostages, including Petty Officer Stethem, Marine Lt. Col. Higgins, and diplomat William Buckley. More important, this knowledge may help us to avoid future losses.

Effectiveness of Modern Assassins

On his deathbed, Hassan is reputed to have told his faithful followers, "Remember, my spirit is vigilant!"[7] The fida'i of the terrorist ranks of today appear to us as overzealous fanatics taking great personal risks and sometimes dying for their cause. The terrorist "kill ratio" from their suicide bomb attacks has been considerable and largely in their favor. Suicide attacks against U.S. interests began with the April 1983 American embassy bombing by Islamic Jihad, which cost sixty-three lives, seventeen of whom were American. These attacks peaked with the deaths of 241 Marines killed in the October 1983 barracks bombing, and tapered when an American soldier and sailor died in the September 1984 bombing of the embassy annex in Beirut.

Suicide bombing has been greatly emphasized by the press, as well as by the terrorists in their pursuit of violence for effect. Because we are so unfamiliar with such bizarre behavior, the psychological effect of a suicide attack adds enormously to its tactical impact. The subsequent threat of more embassy bombings by a Lebanese military leader in 1989 was all it took to make the United States withdraw the remaining skeleton staff.

Despite their considerable impact, largely because of the enormous media play they receive, Middle Eastern terrorist operations, including the TWA flight 847 and *Achille Lauro* hijackings, are often poorly planned and executed. Originally, there were to have been three hijackers aboard TWA flight

847, but the one who spoke English missed the flight from Athens. He was picked up later when his two compatriots forced the plane to fly to Tunis. The terrorists appeared to have no plan of action after the initial hijacking. The passengers and crew reported that the terrorists often seemed confused and not sure what to do next. This may explain why the airplane flew aimlessly back and forth over the Mediterranean until finally settling down in Beirut. The hijackers appeared never to have flown before and were remarkably ignorant of basic aircraft procedures. They repeatedly demanded the plane fly a distance much greater than its fuel range.

Similarly, there was never any intention to hijack the *Achille Lauro*. The hijackers planned to ride it into an Israeli port and blow up fuel stores. Discovered by a steward while they were talking loudly and cleaning their weapons in their cabin, however, the terrorists took impulsive and unplanned action. Their murder of Leon Klinghofer, a helpless man in a wheelchair, did nothing to advance their cause. It was pointless, brutal, and typical of the poor planning and organization of some terrorist groups.

No matter how poorly educated and trained, the modern Middle Eastern terrorist can be extremely dangerous and deadly. Today, as in the eleventh century, the legacy of Hassan al ibn Sabbah provides a prevailing characteristic of terrorism in the Middle East: "There is . . . the illusion that murder committed for political or religious purposes is an enabling act."[8]

WESTERN EUROPE

The Reign of Terror

Terrorism is not confined to small, radical groups struggling against an oppressive government. Governments themselves use "enforcement terrorism" to control the populace and to prevent revolution. In the eighteenth century during the French Revolution, Maximilien Robespierre and the Jacobins sent numerous aristocrats and other citizens to the guillotine in the name of their social ideals. Modern totalitarian leaders have tried to stay in power with such a reign of terror by suppressing revolution. François (Papa Doc) Duvalier of Haiti, Idi Amin of Uganda, the Shah of Iran, and many Latin American dictators are familiar modern examples. During the Stalinist era, the Soviet Union used enforcement terrorism carried out by the State Security Committee (KGB) against its own citizens. Its tactics included the requirement for internal passports, restriction of travel, detention and interrogation without probable cause or due process, execution without trial, and exile to the gulags.

Theorists of Terrorism

By the nineteenth century, revolutionaries were beginning to theorize and write about terrorism. Many European terrorists of the time were idealistic revolutionaries who wanted violent change but who knew little about the practical means to achieve it. New practices were initiated, such as Wilhelm Weitling's use of criminals in terrorists' ranks in Germany. Criminals were already skilled in the use of weapons, bombs, forgery, theft, assassination, and kidnapping and readily applied these skills to terrorism and revolution.

German terrorist Karl Heinzen advocated the doctrine of the *art of murder* to improve the effectiveness of terrorism, as well as the use of the new technology of the Industrial Revolution for bomb and weapon development.

Johann Most, a German terrorist who was active in the U.S. labor movement, also taught revolutionary technology and is credited with developing the letter bomb. He was one of the first to recognize the significance of the media to terrorism. His concept, *propaganda of the deed*, emphasized that the news of a terrorist event was more important than the event itself. Most's idea reflected the ancient Chinese definition of terrorism: "to kill one and frighten ten thousand others." He understood that the media spread and amplified the impact of violence against selected persons, which made the effect of a terrorist act on the larger audience of greater value to the terrorist cause than simply eliminating the victim. Propaganda of the deed is even more potent for terrorists today because of nearly instantaneous, worldwide television and newspaper coverage of such events.

This essential, vital linkage between terrorism and the media that Most envisioned is the primary force and focus of modern terrorists. To paraphrase Winston Churchill, seldom in the course of history have we seen so few with so little affect so many. Propaganda of the deed is a major problem for counterterrorism policy and planning today.

Revolutionary Catechism

The most chilling theoretical document of the nineteenth century was written by the Russian nihilists Mikhail Bakunin and Serge Nechaev. Consisting of twenty-six articles, *Revolutionary Catechism* delineates the duties and dictates the attitudes of the dedicated revolutionary as a person without feeling, family, or personal ties, whose only goal is the destruction of the established order and who deliberately manipulates and uses others to obtain his anarchistic ends. Although this ideal Russian revolutionary is not suicidal in the sense of the Islamic terrorists, he is willing to live and die for his chaotic cause:

> Every revolutionary must be a dedicated man. He should have no personal affairs, no business, no emotions, no at-

tachments, no property, no name. All these must be wholly absorbed in the single thought and the single passion for revolution. . . .

The revolutionary knows that in the very depths of his being he has broken all ties with society, both in word and in deed. He breaks all ties with the civilized world, its laws, its customs, its morality, all those conventions generally accepted by the world. He is their implacable enemy, and if he has intercourse with the world, it is only for the purpose of destroying it. . . .

Tyrannical towards himself, the revolutionary must be tyrannical towards others. All the emotions that move human beings, all the soft and enervating feelings of kinship, love, friendship, gratitude and honor, must give way to a cold and single-minded passion for revolution. . . . Night and day he must have but one thought, but one aim—merciless destruction. . . .

The revolutionary . . . lives in this world only because he has faith in its quick and complete destruction. He no longer remains a revolutionary if he keeps faith with anything in this world. *He should not hesitate to destroy any position, any place, or any man in this world.*[9] (Italics in the original.)

The apparent purpose of all this isolation from friends and family, manipulation, cold-blooded killing, and wholesale destruction is the "emancipation and happiness" of the laborers of Russia:

The purpose of our society is the entire emancipation and happiness of the people, namely laborers. We are convinced that this happiness can only come about as a result of an all-destroying popular revolt. . . . The only revolution which can do any good to the people is that which destroys, from top to bottom, every idea of state, overthrowing all traditions, social orders, and classes in Russia. . . . Our task is terrible, total, inexorable, and universal destruction![10]

"The people" are ubiquitous in revolutionary and terrorist rhetoric; horrendous deeds have been undertaken in their name. What the people really think of all that was carried out for their supposed benefit is clear today as the Russian revolution has bared the sickness of its soul and communist dictatorships have crumbled throughout the former Soviet Union and in Eastern Europe.

95

Whether *Revolutionary Catechism* is idealism or autobiography, it describes a widespread condition of individual alienation, anomie, fatalism, and nihilism among disaffected Russian (and European) intellectuals of the nineteenth century that led to many revolutionary attempts against the czars. Later, the European radicals, terrorists, and revolutionaries of the 1960s and 1970s displayed similar attitudes and feelings.

The Paradox of Placation

The Narodnoya Volna (People's Will), a late nineteenth-century Russian revolutionary group, followed the *Revolutionary Catechism* and killed Czar Alexander II with a bomb. This act was a demonstration of the paradoxical terrorist principle of death to reformers in order to preserve the revolution. Terrorists often call for reform through revolution, but what they actually want is revolution. The reforms they shout about may be little more than rhetoric designed to garner a wider base of support among the people. A government or political leader who gives in to their demands and brings about needed reforms, possibly even those they have asked for, undermines their revolution and runs the risk of assassination.

Czar Alexander II had begun numerous changes in land reform, political representation, property ownership, and other institutions. These democratic principles, virtually absent in Russia for generations, had been much demanded by radical and revolutionary groups. To kill this reformist czar might seem to be biting the hand that feeds you. From a terrorist perspective, such reforms by the hated establishment kindle hope among the people, reduce their frustration and rage, and, consequently, diminish their support for revolution. Not to kill the czar would have been tantamount to giving up the revolution. Revolution (and terrorism) may have a frightening autonomy, a need to fulfill itself through violence and death, regardless of changes in the societal conditions that gave it birth.

The paradox of placation contributed to the death of Czar Alexander II in nineteenth-century Russia. This paradoxical principle brought about a terrorist bloodbath in twentieth-century Spain when a liberal prince lifted the repressions of a fascist military dictator. The Spanish prince Juan Carlos was crowned after the long, strict military dictatorship of Generalissimo Francisco Franco. Contrary to Franco's oppressive policies, Juan Carlos made many concessions long demanded by the ETA Basque separatists, short of allowing the Basque region to become an independent country. He gave the Basques representation in the Spanish parliament and land reform, permitted them to speak their own language and teach it in their schools, and met a variety of other demands.

Paradoxically, and contrary to everyone's expectation, the ETA (which stands for "Basque Fatherland and Freedom" in the Basque language) terrorists went on a rampage of killing and bombing that was the worst in their long, destructive history. In spite of their rhetoric, the terrorists did not want concessions and greater freedoms. They wanted violence, revolution, and independence. The placating actions of Juan Carlos undermined the Basque revolution and the secession they desired. Their campaign of terror was an expression of rage and frustration and, politically, an effort to rekindle the rebellious spirit of the people in order to foment a revolution.

This paradoxical principle of increased violence and destructiveness in the face of satisfaction of terrorist demands has been illustrated repeatedly in the history of terrorism. Does it have predictive value?

97

The profound political changes taking place in Europe—open borders, reunification of East and West, and, most importantly, the decreasing NATO and U.S. military presence throughout Europe—come very close to meeting the avowed political and social changes that have been sought by terrorists and other radical and liberal groups for many years. Are these changes likely to lessen terrorism in Europe?

Many people would like to believe this will occur; however, if we are to learn the lessons of history, we must be prepared for an even greater level of European terrorism than we have experienced so far. Open borders and reunification make it easier for terrorists to move from country to country in cooperative operations within their destructive terror network. Although the blessings of peace, cooperation, and understanding would appear to reduce the threat of war and revolution, they may also open the door to a tragic increase in terrorist violence and destruction. A similar concern exists for the Middle East peace process, which is likely to be protracted, conflicted, and a focus of terrorist acts by a variety of groups.

Social and Psychological Influences

Attempted revolutions and the terrorist acts that accompany them appear to have a functional autonomy of their own.

Even when reforms are instituted or revolutionary demands are met, terrorist acts of violence continue. The autonomy of these acts is likely the result of several factors. Contrary to their rhetoric, political change is seldom the only goal of most terrorists. Violence for its own sake, the pleasure of destructiveness, the intoxication of power, and the thrill of wielding the sword of fear must be factors.

In addition, violence serves terrorists in a personal way as a vent for their frustration and fury, regardless of its source. Much terrorist rage expressed in violent acts against innocent victims follows the psychological mechanisms of displacement, more popularly called scapegoating. The terrorist who beat and later killed Robert Stethem during the hijacking of TWA flight 847 was clearly displacing his fury over the death of his family onto this innocent sailor. Of course, neither Stethem nor the other military personnel who were beaten and threatened with death had anything to do with the USS *New Jersey's* shelling of Beirut. Similar trends are apparent in the violence of neo-Nazi terrorists groups in Germany today, which seem more like the wanton destructiveness of street gangs than the politically motivated acts of ideological terrorists. The psychological needs served by terrorist violence—the gratifications of expressing hatred and inflicting pain—have been insufficiently studied.

The terrorists' image and life-style are other factors in the autonomy of these acts. Once terrorists have started on a path of violence, it is difficult for them to quit because of pressures from within their own organization and the need to maintain a reputation among other groups. Also, like much deviant social behavior, it is difficult for a person to stop it. Violent crime of any type is a demanding mistress; few abandon her with impunity. The life of a terrorist becomes so estranged from society's norm that the pressures to maintain and continue violent behavior are enormous. The few known terrorists who have abandoned their activities report great difficulty in doing so; others have been killed in the attempt by their own groups.

Modern European Targets and Goals

The stable democracies of modern Europe have made revolution difficult. This fact may help to account for the diligence of European terrorists. U.S. Army ITAC statistics show that about 25 percent of worldwide terrorist activity takes place in Europe; this figure has been consistent throughout the last decade. Although the goals of European terrorists have been rarely achieved, their actions have been particularly aimed at changes in governmental politics or policy, at NATO facilities in attempts to eliminate the Western military presence in Europe, and at American business enterprises.

In contrast to their Middle Eastern counterparts, European terrorists do not primarily attack persons. For instance, the Revolutionary Cells (RZ) of Germany have frequently bombed government buildings and American businesses, but they do so mainly at night, apparently to minimize loss of life. European terrorist groups generally have bombed facilities that are symbolic of their ideological hatred. One aim of the terrorists' actions, and perhaps a reason for their restraint, has been to garner support from the radical segment of the European peace movement that might condone destruction of property in violent protest but not loss of life.

The Transnational Network

No known state sponsorship of terrorism exists within Europe, as it does in the Middle East. Faced with limited resources, European terrorists have had to work together. Although the Red Brigades have operated mainly in Italy and the Red Army Faction in Germany, one aspect of their operations is a joint, transnational history. Working with other groups offers a wider range of experience, training, weapons, cash, operational skills, safe houses, and the like.

100

The 1972 Lod (Israel) Airport massacre demonstrated both the existence of a complex terror network in Europe and the high level of destructiveness such an unholy alliance can attain. The Japanese Red Army (JRA) agreed to repay the Popular Front for the Liberation of Palestine (PFLP) for training they had received at PFLP camps in Lebanon by conducting a murderous attack against the Israelis. Czechoslovakian-made weapons were delivered by Algerian diplomatic pouch to three JRA terrorists in Italy who had traveled from Japan via Canada to conduct the assault on the Israeli airport. Cash for the operation was obtained from Libya and delivered to the JRA in Belgium. The JRA operatives flew from Rome to Tel Aviv on an Air France jet. They unleashed their assault rifles and Soviet hand grenades in the baggage claim area of Lod Airport with the intention of killing Israelis from an El Al flight. Ironically, in the confusion, they killed twenty-six tourists, mostly Puerto Ricans, and injured more than seventy others who were visiting the Holy Land to celebrate Easter. Two JRA terrorists were killed or committed suicide; the third survived and was jailed for life.

European Terrorist Profile of the 1960s and 1970s

Until the late 1970s, European terrorists often were from the middle to wealthy classes, in their mid-twenties to mid-thirties, college educated, and politically knowledgeable. Usually, they had been radicalized while in college and recruited by terrorist organizations offering these idealists the means to satisfy their utopian dreams. Many of these radical intellectuals lacked operational skills, and criminals began to find their way into the terrorist ranks.

During this era, terrorism was an equal opportunity employer that not only recruited women but often placed them in high leadership positions. Fusako Shigenobu was one of the JRA's top planners and strategists, and Lila Khalid became second in command of the PFLP. Ulrike Marie Meinhoff, in her mid-forties and college educated, was a respected journalist and a secret member of the Communist party in Germany. She became the "founding mother" of the Baader-Meinhoff gang, the name the press gave the so-called Red Army Faction.

European terrorists were typically the most educated and highly trained at that time. Their operations were planned well, executed with precision, and had a political purpose. In ironic contrast to the violence of their actions, the goal of many German and Italian terrorist operations was the elimination of the U.S. and NATO military presence in Europe, and they tried to appeal to the peace and antinuclear movements. Much has changed in European terrorism, however, since the 1960s and 1970s.

Profile Changes since the 1980s

The founders and ideological leaders of most European terrorist groups are dead or in prison. The new members are not as well educated and seem to have little political awareness, but they are often more violent. Many are hoodlums from street gangs. Their aims and politics are unclear; they seem to be involved in violence for its own sake. This description is particularly true of the increasing right-wing threat of neo-Nazi terrorism, especially in Germany. Following the suicide of Rudolph Hess, the last imprisoned Nazi war criminal, right-wing groups undertook an extensive and destructive bombing campaign—a puerile expression of rage over the death of one of their last heroes. The well-educated, radical, politically aware ideological terrorists of the 1970s have passed into history, but their legacy of violence continues to live and grow.[11]

102

LATIN AMERICA

The Modern Revolutionary

Terrorists in this part of the world are responsible for more than one-half of all worldwide terrorist incidents, according to U.S. Army ITAC statistics. The U.S. military presence has increased in Latin America during the past decade. Its operations have included interdicting drug traffickers (Colombia, Bolivia, and Peru), advising (Honduras and El Salvador), invasion (Panama) and counterinsurgency (Nicaragua). Numerous civilians and military personnel have died; others have been taken hostage. Latin American terrorism against U.S. interests can be expected to increase in direct proportion to political and military involvement of the United States in that area.

Latin American terrorism is not as widely recognized nor does it receive the same media attention as Middle Eastern operations. It differs in significant respects from terrorism almost anywhere else in the world. Most Latin American terrorists are engaged in full-scale revolution. They are not alienated radicals lashing out at the system, angry juvenile delinquents expressing their frustrations through violence and destruction, or illiterate fundamentalist religious fanatics engaged in self-proclaimed "holy" wars.

Latin American revolutionaries generally live in deeply divided societies. The rich and powerful minority controls the government, operates the businesses, owns the land, and reaps the profits. The poor and helpless majority work the land and live in grinding poverty. Latin terrorists want nothing less than to redress this inequity, overhaul the social order, and redistribute the wealth—or so they say. Their success, however, seems to follow Ambrose Bierce's definition of revolution as "an abrupt change in the form of misgovernment."[12]

103

Profile of the Latin American Terrorist

Latin American terrorists are educated about political revolutions, guerrilla warfare, and the tactics and strategy of terrorism. Some have become modern theorists and writers about terrorist tactics, including Cuban Ché Guevarra and Brazilian Carlos Marighella with his *Mini-Manual of the Urban Guerrilla.* Usually, these terrorists have a constituency and a popular cause. They have a hope of winning, thanks largely to the unstable and corrupt governments they are trying to topple. They have had successful revolutions in Cuba and, until recently, Nicaragua; they have steadily become a potent political force in El Salvador.

Although many Latin American terrorist groups are Marxist-Leninist, they do not appear to be necessarily anti-American. After all, their goal is insurgency—to bring about civil war in their own countries. They have little interest in and less to gain from picking a fight with the United States. Consequently, they seem to attack U.S. interests when they perceive that the United States is interfering with their revolutions. For example, El Salvador had few anti-American terrorist attacks until U.S. military advisers were sent there to train the Salvadoran military in counterinsurgency tactics. The United States then became identified with the enemy the terrorists were trying to overthrow. Although U.S. military advisers operated with a low profile, wore no uniforms or rank insignia, and were trained to avoid terrorist assaults, several military members were killed during recent years. The Salvadoran insurgents, members of the FMLN, assassinated a U.S. Navy military adviser, SEAL Lt. Commdr. Al Schaufleberger, in 1983. During 1985, they killed two American businessmen and four Marine embassy guards who were at an off-limits club. These attacks and others were intended to send a message to the United States that its military interference was not going to be tolerated.

104

Terrorism and the Revolutionary Formula

The formula used in many attempted and successful revolutions is quite simple. Although Marx and Lenin did not invent the formula, it usually bears their names. Their Communist followers, attempting to foment a revolution or war of national liberation in their own countries, often attribute the formula to Marx and Lenin because of its application during the Russian Revolution. Terrorism is intended to be only the initial part of this revolutionary process. Terrorists in many countries seldom get farther than this first step for many reasons—lack of resources, insufficient popular support, a stable, resilient host government, or little interest in more than the hit-and-run violence of terrorism for its own sake. In Latin America, however, terrorism has often been a route to insurgency. All steps of the revolutionary formula, as listed below, have been applied with chilling success:

• Terrorist attacks begin with bombing, hostage-taking, or assassination. Selected targets have symbolic importance, high visibility, and social impact, such as government figures, business leaders, police, judges, military—those who support the system or the status quo.

• The attacks make the government appear inept and unable to protect the people, which causes anxiety and divisiveness among them.

• The attacks also make the terrorists appear omnipotent and invincible: "We can get anyone, anytime, anywhere."

• The contrast between the seeming weakness of the government and the apparent power of the terrorists enables the terrorists to gain group support and cohesion through the effectiveness of their actions.

105

• The attacks produce further government overreaction, resulting in martial law, repression, censorship, mass arrests, trials without due process, and loss of freedoms and civil rights.

• Severe government repression triggered by repeated terrorist assaults creates the proper climate for revolution among the people.[13]

Case Examples of El Salvador and Nicaragua

In the late 1970s, El Salvador had as many as thirty-two different leftist groups vying with the government for recognition and power. By the early 1980s, as a result of the effective joint terrorist actions of several of them, these disparate groups had cohered and coalesced into a single, five-part organization under one aegis, the FMLN. As its power and local support increased, the FMLN moved from sporadic terrorist attacks to guerrilla warfare and then to civil war against the shaky and divided government. Today, the FMLN is a force to be reckoned with in El Salvador. It has won concessions from the government and is involved in peace talks and power sharing. The FMLN has a political position. Its members are permitted to express their views without censorship and have been on the ballot in local elections. Terrorism was a successful route to insurgency and political representation for the FMLN.

In Nicaragua, a similar pattern was followed by the Sandinista revolutionaries. The corrupt and dictatorial Somoza regime refused to share power. The communist Sandinistas, following the same formula used by the FMLN, began with terrorism and ended with civil war in which they were able to overthrow Somoza, drive him out of the country, and eventually assassinate him.

The purest cases of terrorism as just an initial tactic in an overall strategy of insurgency are found in Latin America. In addition, Latin America accounts for better than half of the world's terrorist activity. This significant strategic fact seems to have been eclipsed by the actions of Middle Eastern terrorists who have achieved superior press relations and by the U.S. government's preoccupation with the Middle East peace process.

In recent years, Latin American terrorists have become more involved with the drug cartels, especially in Colombia, Peru, and Bolivia. As the U.S. military becomes more active in the war on drugs south of the border, it will encounter increasing amounts of violence from both the terrorists and the drug operators. The United States must wake up to the obvious presence and the danger of Latin American terrorism and cease to ignore this "sleeping giant" at its doorstep.

THE LESSONS OF TERRORISM

Terrorism is the lowest rung on the revolutionary ladder. Some groups do not climb beyond this rung. Terrorism is all they care to do or all they are able to do because the governments they attack are too stable and secure to be toppled. With its weaponry and level of destructiveness, however, terrorism can have a tremendous social and political impact.

We must consider the geopolitical, cultural, and historical

settings of terrorism to understand it in its proper context. A single terrorist act, taken out of context as the media repeatedly does, makes little sense, especially when compared with similar acts in other parts of the world. It could be argued that a killing is a killing is a killing. . . . A terrorist assault may be a senseless act of violence and therefore meaningless and unpredictable. If we see it that way and react only to the act itself, torn from context, we have few options but to revile the perpetrators, plot revenge, and perpetuate the vicious cycle of attack and counterattack. More often, a terrorist act is a political and social statement. It might be an expression of revengeful, religious fervor in the Middle East; an effort to drive NATO forces from Europe; or the result of U.S. interference in Latin American civil affairs. Although the act is still destructive, context gives it meaning.

Through an understanding of the context and meaning of terrorist activities can come better predictability, improved assessment of threats, and an increased degree of control. Most importantly, understanding can enhance the possibility of achieving constructive action. If we are to progress in dealing with terrorism and not fall victim to Santayana's fatalistic prophecy, we must become aware of the manifold differences in the geopolitical context and meaning of terrorism around the globe. This understanding is a necessary foundation of the policy, diplomacy, and commitment to a firm, proactive stance required to ameliorate the political circumstances and social conditions that foster terrorism.

CHAPTER 6

Social Issues of Terrorism

Can we foresee an end to terrorism? More than two thousand years of history say no. Terrorism is tyranny by the weak and disenfranchised. Much of its appeal comes from its effectiveness, efficiency, ease, and usefulness. Even if the political and social changes now taking place in Europe and the Middle East eventually spell an end to terrorism in those areas, it will continue to be widely practiced in Latin America and other parts of the world.

Terrorism is a powerful tool for the powerless. Almost all revolutions, including the American Revolution, began with terrorism. The Boston Tea Party, for instance, was a successful step for the American colonies. Terrorism will continue to be used by groups that are trying to foment civil war or that feel they have no other option to publicize their cause or concerns. Especially today, the temptations offered by instant, worldwide electronic media coverage of their acts are too much for most terrorists to ignore.

TECHNOLOGY AND CONSTRAINTS
ON TERRORISM

Terrorism has a banal repetitiveness about it because it has changed little throughout its history. The goals, aims, rhetoric, tactics, and success (or nonsuccess) of terrorism have remained essentially unchanged and make it quite predictable. The only *un*predictable thing about terrorism is when and where the next strike will occur. Technological advances, however, have changed the *methods* of terrorists. Weapons and bombs have become more sophisticated. The media impact of terrorism is more powerful and immediate, not because of how terrorists use the media, but simply because of technological innovations. Terrorists have little need to escalate their level of violence and destructiveness as long as they feel their actions get the publicity and result in the social and political impact they want.

The use of terrorist violence requires important constraints. When terrorists try to publicize certain social inequities or government oppression, they must act in a manner that does not make them appear to be the oppressors. If they try to appeal to peace or antinuclear groups, most of whom condone only minimal aggressiveness to publicize their views, terrorists must be careful that their own aggression does not boomerang and cause them loss of support.

Concern that its violence had gone too far and alienated some of its supporters apparently prompted the Irish Republican Army (IRA) to apologize for the Christmas bombing of Harrod's department store in London. The IRA has usually attacked British police and military personnel in what it regards as its war for independence. The Harrod's bombing killed and injured civilian women and children who constituted no military threat to the IRA. This may have been more than many of its supporters could tolerate. The IRA issued a public apology in an apparent effort to win back those supporters. Evidently, it recognized the boomerang effect of excessive violence.

The intent or motive of a terrorist action can be a predictor of the level of violence to which the terrorists will resort. If their motives are mainly publicity or politics, the violence is likely to be more controlled. Extreme violence can result in bad publicity, and the terrorists may alienate those to whom they are trying to appeal. Terrorist acts in this category have usually involved only a few deaths and sometimes no more than one. RAND Corporation terrorism expert Brian Jenkins has commented that "incidents of mass murder are truly rare. . . . Terrorists want a lot of people *watching*, not a lot of people *dead*."[1]

On the other hand, if terrorists are motivated by revenge or retribution, their level of violence can be much greater and, accordingly, the death toll may be higher. By blowing up Pan Am flight 103 and killing a total of 276 people, the terrorists apparently intended retribution for the shooting down of an Iranian airliner by the USS *Vincennes*, in which a comparable number of people died.

Nuclear, Biological, and Chemical Terrorism

From the perspective of terrorists, there is little point in their attempting the great technical complexities of nuclear, biological, or chemical (NBC) terrorism when the conventional approach works so well. Also, NBC methods involve substantial hazards to the terrorists themselves. Conventional explosives and weaponry are dangerous enough. Several terrorists have been killed or maimed while working with explosives and homemade bombs. A member of a notorious Puerto Rican terrorist group, Armed Forces for National Liberation (FALN), blew his hands off and injured his face during his bomb-making activities. Few terrorists have the high level of technical expertise, knowledge, competence, and skill required to handle NBC weapons.

Some extremist governments, such as Libya, Iran, and Iraq, who support and sponsor terrorism have doubtless considered providing their terrorist operatives with NBC weapons. Each of these governments has been attempting to develop a nuclear weapons capability and has learned how difficult that is. Iraq has developed and used chemical weapons on its own people and in the war with Iran. Iraq may have been constrained in their use against allied troops during Desert Storm because of the strong pressures of world public opinion. Also, Iraq may have previously discovered that chemical weapons are difficult to develop, handle, transport, and use so they do not present a hazard to its own troops. NBC weapons have a built-in boomerang effect.

Use of the Media

Although terrorists have had little success in causing lasting political change, they have been enormously effective in their manipulation of the press and preemption of other news. Publicity and media attention have become so desirable and necessary to terrorists that they often appear to neglect, disregard, or subvert their political goals in pursuit of publicity.

Americans want to know about world events and rely on the news media to keep them informed. When a terrorist action takes place, it may seem that the press is simply reporting the news, but the extent to which terrorists have enticed the media into playing their political game is readily apparent. Manipulating the media, maintaining a grip for as long as needed, and using the power of the press are basic to the operational strategy and tactics of terrorism.

WE ARE ALL THE TARGET

During the 1985 hijacking of TWA flight 847 to Beirut, previously unknown local politicians became overnight international figures. (What has been heard about Nabih Berri lately?) Hooded terrorists became the guests, via satellite, of morning talk show hosts. Former hostages were turned into heroes and celebrities before and after they returned home. More recently, entire news broadcasts have been devoted to "the situation in Iraq" (or Beirut or Tehran) and the "shadowy groups behind the bombings and kidnappings."

In our reactions to terrorism, we often lose our perspective and sense of proportion. Regardless of the actual number of casualties, terrorist attacks seem especially painful and appalling to us because of the propaganda of the deed conveyed by the media. Compared with other forms of violence and death in our society, terrorist attacks are much less destructive. Many more people are killed in traffic accidents or by criminal homicides or snake bites in the United States each year than are killed by terrorists throughout the world. As measured by actual loss of life, automobile accidents, homicides, and snakes are greater social problems. Yet, nowhere does one hear the public outcry or observe the political reaction that results from terrorist acts because these causes of death do not claim the media appeal and public attention of terrorism.

Too often and too intently, the medium of television has become the surrogate of terrorism—supporting, aiding, and abetting the terrorists by pandering to its own needs to attract viewers and sell advertising products and to terrorists' need to hold people hostage to their TV sets. Ignorance was understandable in the early years of terrorism's manipulation of the media, but not now. Clearly, terrorism sells. The product being sold is the suffering of Americans, with the economic profits going to the media and the political profits to the terrorists.

Terrorism is truly the mouse that roared. Its destructiveness is relatively minor compared with other social problems. Yet, the psychological impact is enormous because of the way in which these events are reported. In fact, terrorism would be impotent without the instantaneous, worldwide publicity provided by the media.

113

Following the resolution of the 1985 hijacking of TWA flight 847, the media held several publicly televised discussions of their coverage of this event. I was hopeful that they would look carefully at their excesses, realize the extent to which they had pandered to the terrorists and supported their cause, and realize that the coverage had seriously threatened the lives of all those who went through the ordeal. I had also hoped that they would invite others, who were not with the media, to participate in these discussions. Members of the State Department with terrorism experience and perhaps some former hostages would have been good choices. None of my hopes were realized. The televised discussions maintained a thin veneer of serious analysis and discussion, but the cronyism and self-congratulation were obvious. The media decided that the media had done just fine.

In a country that prides itself on free speech and whose rights in that regard are guaranteed by the First Amendment of the Constitution, it is quite difficult to consider any restraint on the media, no matter how reasonable. Certainly, the press itself and most Americans are against media censorship.

Although self-imposed media restraint and peer review have not adequately solved the problem, some moderation and a less sensationalist approach to reporting terrorist events have been apparent since the hijacking of TWA flight 847. Perhaps the media have become more aware of how they have been used to further terrorists' interests in publicity and propaganda. Because there has been no similar hijacking since 1985, perhaps what appears to be self-restraint is really lack of opportunity. The likelihood of future hijacking of international flights is high. It remains to be seen how the media will respond.

114

THE LIMITS OF SECURITY

During the past three decades of terrorism, increased security measures have greatly improved the public's safety. With high-technology electronic screening of passengers and their baggage, the Federal Bureau of Investigation and Federal Aviation Administration have virtually eliminated domestic hijacking from U.S. airports. Hijacking and bombing continue to be problems in other countries, but they have lessened over the years. Better police cooperation across national borders, sharing of computer files on known terrorists and criminals, and improved methods of profiling have increased passenger safety.

Embassies, military bases, ships, squadrons, and civilian corporations located in foreign countries have also improved their security so that the personnel of these organizations can feel safer at work. Unfortunately, these improvements may lead some people to a false sense of security because of their organizational dependency. Organizations do provide increased safety under their protective umbrellas, but it is unwise to relax personal precautions. Security is an individual responsibility. Most terrorist assaults occur when victims are away from the security of their organizations.

Terrorists have reacted to the increased organizational security of certain targets by shifting to easier ones. For instance, as U.S. military bases in Europe have hardened themselves, terrorists have shifted their attacks to softer, more vulnerable targets. Examples include the bombing of bars popular with American service personnel in Athens by the National Front (February 1985) and in Madrid by the Islamic Jihad (April 1985), of the U.S. military post exchange in Frankfurt (November 1985), and of a discotheque frequented by U.S. service personnel in Berlin (April 1986). Terrorists will *always* move toward softer targets. When it was too tough to hijack or blow up an Israeli airliner, they machine-gunned Jewish and other passengers in the terminal buildings (Rome and Vienna airport massacres, December 1985). As security has increased around military, diplomatic, and corporate targets, terrorists have attacked social and recreational centers.

Greater security does not solve the problem of terrorism; it merely shifts the target locus. This makes it particularly important that individuals take an even greater interest in and become thoroughly knowledgeable about their own security. Any persons at risk can never know too much about personal protection and hostage survival.

ACCEPTABLE RISKS

We must accept the fact that the world is not our backyard. We cannot expect to be safe, protected, and privileged by virtue of being American. There are places to which we can no longer travel with prudence and impunity. If we do, we must accept certain risks and possible casualties. We must acknowledge the danger of working in or traveling to unsafe countries. Our government will not always be able to rescue or aid us if we get into trouble. Former President Ronald Reagan said as much. Unfortunately, this advice is realistic in today's world.

The rest of us who remain at home must also accept this fact. Americans are in other countries largely by their own choice. We should not overreact when they are taken hostage or killed by terrorists, even though we have long held to the value of human life. We should not temporize about that value now, but we must realize that it is also an Achilles heel through which terrorists repeatedly strive to exploit and control us.

116
———

Perhaps we should regard Americans who choose to travel or work in dangerous areas of the globe as volunteer soldiers in battle. If they are captured or killed, we should allow the government or military authorities to handle the incidents as quietly and effectively as possible—without media involvement, without fanfare, without public grief, without publicity for the terrorists.

When Americans are taken hostage, they deserve all we can *reasonably* give to negotiate for them, try to rescue them, or mourn them. But, if they voluntarily risk their own lives by going into dangerous zones through personal choice and are taken hostage, we should not allow our government and the rest of us to be held hostage. The victims should be treated like soldiers who are killed in battle—their families should be given a medal and monetary payment. Let that be the end of it. Perhaps this notion seems cold, crass, and cynical to some; it is not suggested from that perspective. We do not deserve to be exploited because of the choices of a few. When the government no longer permits Americans to be highly valued pawns in the terrorist game of international extortion, the terrorists will stop kidnapping Americans. In fighting terrorism, we must be willing to make some sacrifices that will provide the greatest good for the greatest number.

COUNTERATTACKS

Launch a Personal Boycott

Economic boycotts of countries that shelter, support, and foster terrorism have been considered by the U.S. government. In the complex, interlocking economic realities of the world today, allied support for such actions has been difficult to achieve. Individual Americans, however, can and have successfully boycotted such nations with potent impact.

117

Acting in concert as individuals is in keeping with our heritage and democratic values. It enables us to do as citizens what our government does not do. Voting with dollars against terrorism by not traveling to certain countries is both prudent and a powerful message. Whether out of fear for our safety or out of principle, the message is the same: We will not tolerate countries that harbor, encourage, and give comfort to those that seek to exploit, injure, and destroy us.

Because of numerous international terrorist actions in the early 1980s, many American tourists and their dollars went to the Vancouver Expo during the summer of 1986 rather than to countries abroad. Their collective choice caused much distress among European and Middle Eastern nations that had long relied on tourist dollars for much of their income. For example, Egypt was estimated to have lost over five million dollars in tourist revenue. This "voting" with dollars sent a strong message to those nations and was a significant factor in subsequent improvements in their security measures. Economic counterterrorism has worked and can be even more effective to the extent that we consistently refuse to travel to, work in, do business with, or invest in countries that are involved in terrorism.

Speak Firmly . . .

The American historical experience of negotiating with terrorists and arms-for-hostages deals has been well chronicled
by Stansfield Turner, retired U.S. Navy admiral and former
118 director of the Central Intelligence Agency under President
—— Jimmy Carter.[2]

America as a nascent nation first encountered terrorism
in 1785 when Barbary Coast pirates from the states of Tripoli, Tunis, Algiers, and Morocco captured two American
ships and held twenty-one American sailors for ransom. The
Continental Congress was unable to solve this problem,
which fell to George Washington when he became president
four years later. Presidents Washington, John Adams, and
Thomas Jefferson, in turn, made deals with the Barbary
Coast pirates, who by then had taken additional American
hostages. That these pirates were given ransom payments,
arms, a fighting ship, and annual tributes has a strangely
modern ring in light of the Reagan administration's Iran-
contra arms-for-hostages deals.

According to Admiral Turner, "Jimmy Carter was not the
first President to send a rescue force after Americans being
held hostage. In 1805 President Thomas Jefferson dispatched
a ragtag expedition of mercenaries across the desert of Egypt
into the Barbary State of Tripoli to rescue 307 Americans."[3]
While lacking the technical skill and military support of
Delta Force, this expedition at least succeeded in bringing
the opposing forces to the bargaining table where more ransom was paid, although a treaty was signed to end the annual
tribute. By 1815, President James Madison had a larger navy
and was able to exercise a more potent military option to
quell the Barbary pirates once and for all.

Teddy Roosevelt faced a crisis in 1904 that involved only two hostages taken by a descendant of the Barbary Coast pirates. He sent in two navy ships that were mostly ineffective because the hostages were being held in the mountains. He engaged in much anti-terrorist rhetoric and bombast that gave him the historical reputation of being "tough" on terrorism, but he made a quiet deal to get the hostages out.

After the USS *Pueblo* was captured by North Korea in 1968, Lyndon Johnson eventually made a deal to obtain the release of the crew, which had been held for more than a year. Richard Nixon supported a deal between King Hussein of Jordan and the Palestine Liberation Organization (PLO) for the freedom of American hostages after the Popular Front for the Liberation of Palestine (PFLP) hijacked several aircraft to Dawson Field in the desert near Amman, Jordan.

Gerald Ford, alone among modern presidents, did *not* make a deal when confronted with a hostage-taking. In 1975, the U.S. merchant ship *Mayaguez*, with thirty-nine American seaman aboard, was seized by a Cambodian gunboat. President Ford exercised a military option and sent in the Marines. The hostages were freed, but forty-one Marines lost their lives in a helicopter crash. Yet, America judged this a great success and the president's popularity soared.

Terrorism has touched American presidents since the founding of this country. Most have had to negotiate with terrorists; some have made deals. Political rhetoric that shakes a fist or rattles a sabre at terrorists and eschews negotiation, a basic tool of diplomacy, has little value. The United States must be ready to negotiate when our citizens are taken hostage. We also must be ready for forceful intervention, if necessary, and in that order. Our experience with terrorism has shown that the great majority of hostage-takings of all kinds have been resolved by negotiation, and this will continue.

. . . and Carry a Big Stick

The helplessness of Americans when they are confronted by governments that function with a terrorist mentality is nothing new. For years, we denied and tried to ignore the Soviet Union's terrorism against its own citizens under Stalin and even accepted that country as one of our allies in World War II. Similarly, the United States tried to ignore the terrorist tactics of Hitler until we were literally forced to a confrontation.

President Reagan's launch of an air strike against Libya for its state sponsorship of the La Belle Disco bombing in Berlin indicated that times were changing. President George Bush took military and economic action by initiating Operations Desert Shield and Desert Storm against Iraq for invading Kuwait, holding Americans and other civilians hostage, and threatening Saudi Arabia. The combined actions of these presidents made it clear that the United States no longer countenances nations that traffic in terrorism.

Unite the United Nations

The particularly significant factor about Operations Desert Shield and Desert Storm was that the United States did not act alone. The United Nations sanctioned and supported these actions, and many countries participated. For the first time in recent history, international terrorism was hit with an international counterattack.

Although torn by severe domestic and economic problems, the Soviet Union provided ideological and political support against the terrorist actions of Iraq's Saddam Hussein. In itself, the Soviets' stand against terrorism was a noteworthy and significant change. Cooperation between East and West may set the stage and shape the course of history for the rest of the world. For nearly half a century, the most powerful nations on earth exercised their leadership by aiming nuclear missiles and threatening each other (and the entire planet) with extinction. In curbing Saddam's expansionist policies through a measured and controlled response, the world's great powers pulled together in a civilized manner and demonstrated their strength with restraint. Most importantly, for the first time the United States and the Soviet Union acted together as true world leaders.

121

The United States and the Soviet Union may appear to be strange bedfellows against terrorism. As noted in the introduction, however, a serious outbreak of peace had been taking place in Europe. The Soviet Union began to withdraw its troops from the communist bloc nations. One by one, mostly through peaceful revolutions, these nations voted out their dictatorial communist regimes and replaced them with democratic governments. In themselves, these are unprecedented historical events; but what has followed from these changes is even more surprising and would have been unthinkable just a few years ago.

Rapid changes continue. The nascent alliances between the United States and the newly forged republics of the former Soviet Union are altogether different from the cooperation during World War II. For the first time in history, true international cooperation between East and West seems to be an emerging reality that could have a significant impact on reducing terrorism in parts of the world.

The breakup of the Soviet Union, together with the new alliances between the Russian republics and the United States, could result in the withdrawal of political, ideological, military, and economic support of terrorism by client states and surrogates of the former Soviet Union. Many such countries, including Cuba, Nicaragua, Libya, Iraq, Iran, and Syria, have actively practiced and sponsored terrorist activity locally and around the globe with clandestine sanction and support by the Soviet Union. The ability of these countries to engage in widespread terrorism may be severely curtailed without Soviet approval and support. Profound changes taking place in the erstwhile Soviet Union and Warsaw Pact countries could, thus, produce a significant enervation and reduction of terrorism throughout the world.

The new millennium is just ahead. As the twenty-first century looms, do these auspicious signs herald propitious changes to come? The possibility exists that this rapidly changing political climate will produce an abatement of terrorism, as well as an increase in international cooperation toward world peace. Perhaps those who prophesy a new age are correct. For the rest of us, there is hope. We shall see.

Notes

INTRODUCTION

1. Brian Michael Jenkins, "Future Trends in International Terrorism" (paper presented at the Defense Intelligence College, Washington, D.C., 3 December 1985).

2. U.S. Army Intelligence Agency, *Terrorism: The Worldwide Threat and Protective Measures for the US Military (A Briefing) (U)* (Washington, D.C.: U.S. Army Intelligence and Threat Analysis Center, May 1989).

3. Ibid.

4. Stansfield Turner, *Terrorism and Democracy* (Boston: Houghton Mifflin, 1991).

CHAPTER 1

1. Training Staff, *Dynamics of International Terrorism* (Ft. Walton Beach, Fla.: U.S. Air Force Special Operations School, Hurlbut Field, 1982).

2. Naval Investigative Service, "Anti-Terrorism Awareness/ Protective Measures" and "Anti-Terrorism Travel Security Measures" (pamphlets available from CO, NAVFORMPUB-CEN, 5801 Tabor Avenue, Philadelphia, Pa. 19120, and most offices of the Naval Investigative Service).

3. Turner, *Terrorism and Democracy.*

CHAPTER 2

1. Executive Order 10631, "Code of Conduct for Members of the Armed Forces of the United States." 17 August 1955, as amended.

124

2. Ibid., Article V.

3. *Code of Conduct for U.S. Military Personnel,* Department of Defense Directive 1300.7, 23 December 1988.

4. Ibid., Enclosure (3), "Guidance for Instruction to Assist U.S. Military Personnel in Captivity or Hostile Detention during Peacetime."

5. Ibid.

6. Ibid.

7. Ibid.

8. Ibid.

9. Ibid.

10. Ibid.

11. Ibid.

CHAPTER 3

1. Special Agent Supervisor Thomas Strentz, Ph.D., former director of the Behavior Science Unit of the FBI Academy, Quantico, Va., personal communication, 1985.

2. F. M. Ochberg, "A Case Study: Gerald Vaders," in *Victims of Terrorism,* Frank M. Ochberg and David A. Soskis, eds. (Boulder, Colo.: Westview Press, 1982), 9–35.

3. Hans Selye, *The Stress of Life* (revised paperback edition, New York: McGraw-Hill, 1978).

4. Peter Hill with David Friend, "The Angriest Hostage," *Life,* April 1986, 50–64.

5. Brig. Gen. James Dozier, U.S. Army (retired), lecture presented at the Squadron Officers School, Maxwell Air Force Base, Montgomery, Ala., December 1985.

6. Brian Michael Jenkins, Janera Johnson, and David Ronfeldt, *Numbered Lives: Some Statistical Observations from Sev-*

enty-seven International Hostage Episodes (Santa Monica, Calif.: RAND Corporation Report, 1977). This study was cited by Special Agent Frederick J. Lanceley during a lecture presented to the Hostage Negotiation Seminar, FBI Academy, Quantico, Va., August 1985.

7. Jenkins, "Future Trends."

CHAPTER 4

1. Richard H. Rahe and Ellen Genender, "Adaptation to and Recovery from Captivity Stress," *Military Medicine* 148, no. 7 (July 1983), 577–585.

2. Martin Symonds, "Victim Responses to Terror: Understanding and Treatment," in *Victims of Terrorism*, Frank M. Ochberg and David A. Soskis, eds. (Boulder, Colo.: Westview Press, 1982), 95–103.

3. Douglas M. Carson, Directorate of Aerospace Safety, Norton Air Force Base, "Temporal Distortion," *Approach*, June 1982.

4. Selye, *The Stress of Life*.

5. Martin Symonds, as quoted in D. S. Everstine and L. Everstine, *People in Crisis: Strategic Therapeutic Interventions* (New York: Brunner/Mazel, 1983).

6. Rahe and Genender, "Adaptation to and Recovery from Captivity Stress."

7. Symonds, *People in Crisis*.

8. Ibid.

9. Jill Smolowe, "Lives in Limbo." *Time* 138 (16 December 1991), 20–24.

10. Leo Eitinger, "The Effects of Captivity," in *Victims of Terrorism*, Frank M. Ochberg and David A. Soskis, eds. (Boulder, Colo.: Westview Press, 1982), 73–93.

11. Jared Tinklenberg, "Coping with Terrorist Victimization," in *Victims of Terrorism*, Frank M. Ochberg and David A. Soskis, eds. (Boulder, Colo.: Westview Press, 1982), 59–72.

12. Robert L. Woolfolk and Paul M. Lehrer, eds., *Principles and Practice of Stress Management* (New York: Guilford Press, 1984).

CHAPTER 5

1. George Santayana, *Flux and Constancy in Human Nature.* Quoted in *The Oxford Dictionary of Quotations*, 3rd ed. (Oxford: Oxford University Press, 1980), 414.

2. *Dynamics of International Terrorism.*

3. *Political Warfare (Counterinsurgency)*, course presented at U.S. Naval Amphibious Base, Coronado, Calif., 1982.

4. Pico Iyer, "A Mysterious Sect Gave Its Name to Political Murder," *Smithsonian*, 17, no. 7 (October 1986), 145–162.

5. U.S. Army Intelligence Agency, *Terrorism: The Worldwide Threat.*

6. During the August 1985 Hostage Negotiation Seminar at the Federal Bureau of Investigation Academy, Quantico, Va., I had an excellent opportunity to learn the details of what happened during the TWA flight 847 episode from some of the agents who had debriefed the passengers in Beirut. Although Stethem was a large man and physically strong, there was no indication from the reports of the passengers that he had acted in any way to draw the attention of the terrorists or their rage toward him.

7. Iyer, "A Mysterious Sect."

8. Ibid.

9. *Revolutionary Catechism*, as quoted in Robert Payne, *Zero, the Story of Terrorism* (New York: John Day Company, 1950), 7–14.

10. Ibid.

11. "Shift in terrorism finds less idealism, yet more death," *The San Diego Union*, 13 November 1983, A20–A21.

12. Ambrose Bierce, *The Devil's Dictionary* (New York: Dover, 1958). In his definition of revolution, Bierce states, "Revolutions are usually accompanied by a considerable effu-

sion of blood, but are accounted worth it—this appraisement being made by beneficiaries whose blood had not the mischance to be shed."

    13. *Political Warfare (Counterinsurgency).*

CHAPTER 6

    1. Jenkins, "Future Trends."
    2. Turner, *Terrorism and Democracy.*
    3. Ibid.

Index

Index

135

About the Author

Douglas S. Derrer earned his Ph.D. in psychology from Yale University. He worked for the Ford Foundation, the University of California at Santa Cruz, and the University of California Medical Center, San Francisco, before entering the U.S. Navy in 1978 as a clinical psychologist. His tours of duty have included Roosevelt Roads Puerto Rico, SERE School, the Naval Academy, Naval Hospital Camp Pendleton, and Naval Hospital Guam (where he was the Head of the Alcohol Rehabilitation Department). He is a Commander in the Medical Service Corps.

The **Naval Institute Press** is the book-publishing arm of the U.S. Naval Institute, a private, nonprofit professional society for members of the sea services and civilians who share an interest in naval and maritime affairs. Established in 1873 at the U.S. Naval Academy in Annapolis, Maryland, where its offices remain today, the Naval Institute has more than 100,000 members worldwide.

Members of the Naval Institute receive the influential monthly magazine *Proceedings* and discounts on fine nautical prints, ship and aircraft photos, and subscriptions to the quarterly *Naval History* magazine. They also have access to the transcripts of the Institute's Oral History Program and get discounted admission to any of the Institute-sponsored seminars offered around the country.

The Naval Institute's book-publishing program, begun in 1898 with basic guides to naval practices, has broadened its scope in recent years to include books of more general interest. Now the Naval Institute Press publishes more than sixty new titles each year, ranging from how-to books on boating and navigation to battle histories, biographies, ship and aircraft guides, and novels. Institute members receive discounts on the Press's nearly 400 books in print.

Full-time students are eligible for special half-price membership rates. Life memberships are also available.

For a free catalog describing the Naval Institute Press books currently available, and for further information about U.S. Naval Institute membership, please write to:

Membership & Communications Department
U.S. Naval Institute
118 Maryland Avenue
Annapolis, Maryland 21402-5035

Or call, toll-free, (800) 233-8764.

THE NAVAL INSTITUTE PRESS

WE ARE ALL THE TARGET
A Handbook of Terrorism Avoidance and Hostage Survival

Designed by Karen L. White

Set in Bodoni and Futura Extrabold
by BG Composition
Baltimore, Maryland

Printed on 50-lb. Lakewood
and bound by BookCrafters, Inc.
Fredericksburg, Virginia